The Theatre Student

MAKEUP AND MASKS

The Theatre Student

MAKEUP AND MASKS

Ellen Terry
and
Lynne Anderson

PUBLISHED BY
RICHARDS ROSEN PRESS, INC.
NEW YORK, N.Y. 10010

Standard Book Number: 8239–0232–3
Library of Congress Catalog Card Number: 78–139744
Dewey Decimal Classification: 792

Published in 1971 by Richards Rosen Press, Inc.
29 East 21st Street, New York City, N.Y. 10010

First Edition

Manufactured in the United States of America

This book is dedicated with love and thanks to our favorite faces: Mr. and Mrs. Albert E. Terry and Mrs. C. W. Anderson.

ABOUT THE AUTHORS

ELLEN TERRY was born in Provo, Utah, and educated at the Brigham Young University Laboratory and High Schools there. Interested in the theatre from a very early age, she joined the University of Denver summer sessions in theatre for high-school students, then went on to take an A.B. in Dramatic Literature and Criticism from that institution.

Following undergraduate work in Colorado, she went to Yale University, receiving the degree of Master of Fine Arts in Playwriting in 1957.

Since that time, she has been attached to the office of Donald Oenslager, internationally famous theatrical designer and theatre architect, and Columbia Artists Management, Inc., in publicity direction.

Miss Terry has taught Play Production at Barnard College, and Experimental Theatre (Playwriting) at Teachers College, both of Columbia University; has directed and designed for the Westchester Children's Theatre, Dance Arts School; and has been a staff member of the Central City Opera Company, where she obtained her main experience in professional makeup and hairdressing.

She is the author of *Perpetual,* an opera which appeared off-Broadway during the 1963 season, as well as numerous articles, plays, and monographs.

A candidate for a Ph.D. in Speech and Theatre from Columbia University under a Teachers Grant from the Danforth Foundation, Miss Terry has been Associate Professor of Theatre at North Country Community College, Saranac Lake, New York.

LYNNE ANDERSON was born in St. Joseph, Missouri, in 1925. She was graduated from the University of Tulsa in 1948. Her interest in mask-making began there when she helped to create masks for Christopher Marlowe's *Dr. Faustus.*

In 1950 Miss Anderson was granted a two-year graduate fellowship at Smith College, where she studied in the Department of Theatre with Hallie Flanagan Davis. While there she designed and constructed masks for Eugene O'Neill's *The Great God Brown.*

Upon obtaining an M.A. from Smith College, she received a Fulbright grant to study theatrical production in England for the academic year 1952–53. While in England she worked as production and design assistant to several directors and designers at the Old Vic and at the Shakespeare Memorial Theatre, Stratford-on-Avon. In addition to her work in English professional theatre, she made masks for an academic theatre production of Euripides' *Bacchae*.

Returning to the United States, Miss Anderson became Assistant Director of Theatre at MacMurray College in Jacksonville, Illinois. While there she supervised students in the design and construction of masks for Euripides' *Trojan Women*.

Lynne Anderson has written and produced plays for children. One, *A Penny for Your Dreams,* calls for several bird characters to wear masks, and the young actor-dancers designed and made their own masks for this production.

Since obtaining an M.A.L.S. in Library Science at the University of Washington in 1963, Miss Anderson has been working as a media specialist. Currently she is Associate Librarian responsible for media at North Country Community College, Saranac Lake, New York. She has continued her interest in drama and mask-making on a free-lance basis since 1963.

CONTENTS

9

It is so frustrating to walk into a library seeking a comprehensive book on theatrical makeup. Clowns, yes, and for that I'm grateful: all those Halloweens with three sons!

But those country fairs—last summer it was the Strawberry Festival in New Canaan, Connecticut; I completed ninety-nine makeups for children between the hours of 11 and 5, in the rain, yet. And my talents do not lie in that direction. How I wished for simple, ornate patterns, *any* patterns. As it was, they all turned out to be clowns!

So it is with pleasure that I greet this new book by Misses Ellen Terry and Lynne Anderson.

Eileen Heckart
New York, 1970

INTRODUCTION

The actor, like all artists and craftsmen, has many tools at his command. The most important is the play; more specifically, the part he is slated to enact. He also has his body, his voice, and the accouterments of the theatre, such as a stage, his costume, the set, lighting, music, and, of course, an audience relationship.

One of his most important tools is his face. The face is what we observe most closely when first being introduced to a stranger. It is on the face that thoughts, reactions, and emotions stand like words on a page to the sensitive reader. When its owner speaks, the face can serve the same purpose as the orchestra in a concerto: it colors the words with emotional overtones, supports statements, helps to raise questions, and can elucidate irony.

Just as a hammer held too near its head strikes ineffectually, so a misuse of the tool of makeup can mar or even destroy a theatrical performance. Makeup is one of the *crafts* of the theatre; in the hands of a very few, it becomes an art.

With that in mind, we will attempt in this volume to illustrate some guideposts of basic theatrical cosmetic art. Remember, however, that no book, no catalogue, no manual can possibly achieve the same results as disciplined and continuing practice.

From the very dawn of the theatre in our civilization, actors have attempted to change their natural appearance in order to give their audiences heightened aesthetic experiences. It is believed that Thespis and his players colored their faces with the juices of berries and herbs, and we know from painting and sculpture that from the ancient Oriental and Egyptian civilizations on, people have used cosmetics and masks both on- and offstage. The ancient Greeks used masks not only to change their appearance, but also to magnify their voices in the vast amphitheatres.

One of the traditional symbols of the theatre has always been the comic and tragic masks; therefore, no series on the theatre would be complete without a study of the actor's face: real and false.

In their preparation of the bibliography for this volume, the authors found many references to materials, prices, and firms from which they were available. In virtually all cases, such listings were pathetically out-of-date, or irrelevant for foreign purchasers. Not wishing to present material that will be in error within days after publication, the authors have refrained from including lists of materials, prices, and suppliers. It is hoped that the bibliography will be of some use, as published sources of such information will be available in other volumes and continuing periodicals such as *Players Magazine* and *Theatre Crafts*.

To keep abreast of new developments in materials available to the makeup artist and mask-maker, reliable information may be obtained from the American National Theatre and Academy, 245 West 52nd Street, New York, N.Y. 10019, or from the American Educational Theatre Association, 815 17th Street N.W., Washington, D.C. 20006.

The authors gratefully acknowledge the assistance, support, contributions of time, materials, and effort of Dick Smith, S.M.A., Nat Gartsman of CBS-TV, Hap Pekelis of Ashley Famous Agency, A. R. Davidson of Polymer Corporation, Norman Trottier of Hooker-Howe Costume Company, Donald Holden of Watson-Guptill Publications, Charles Grimsley of Missouri Western College, Mr. and Mrs. Wayne E. Vencill, and our ever-patient, ever-kind editor, Dr. Paul Kozelka.

Ellen Terry
Lynne Anderson

Chapter I

THE FACE OF THE ACTOR

"So God created man in His own image, in the image of God created He him; male and female created He them."

Genesis, I:27

Just as an architect would never undertake to design a building without first studying the terrain and general environment in which it was to be built, so an actor must create his makeup "from the ground up," with a thorough knowledge of his own face.

The story is told of a woman who asked her husband, "Do you have a good memory for faces?"

"Yes, I think I do," he replied confidently.

"That's good," said the wife, "because I just broke your shaving mirror."

If you set out upon a systematic study of your own face, you will be amazed at the *new* you to be discovered. Most of us feel we know our own faces quite well, even if we fall short of full Socratic self-knowledge in other respects. But have you ever discovered yourself as a stranger in the shocked moment of confronting a mirror in an unexpected place?

Allowing for the distortions of photography, faulty mirrors, television monitors, and other means of self-appraisal (not the least of which can be the eyes of the beholder), there are ways in which you can learn much about your own face.

To begin, assume the role of the husband in the foregoing story, and test your memory of faces by attempting a self-portrait. Whether you possess drawing ability or not, the chances are you can produce some sort of likeness. Start with the shape around the outside edge and fill in the basic horizontal, vertical, and diagonal planes of your face. Next, attempt the proper spacing and size of your features: eyes, eyebrows, nose, mouth, and ears. Finally, see how much detail you can add: Is that mole by your left or right eye? And just where *is* that scar you bear from a childhood accident? Make one drawing full front and one in profile.

Now look at the subject of your drawing. The chances are your memory of at least one face leaves something to be desired. Inasmuch as viewing one's own profile requires two mirrors and a certain amount of contortion, or at best the use of photography, your drawing is likely to be less than accurate. If you have been ambitious enough to attempt color as well as line, you have probably learned the dismaying fact that your many hundreds of skin tones are virtually impossible to match!

A natural curiosity should arise at this point regarding the why and wherefore of those aspects of your face that escaped your notice, or were forgotten, or that you distorted in your drawing.

You need some rather peculiar equipment for your study of your face and, if

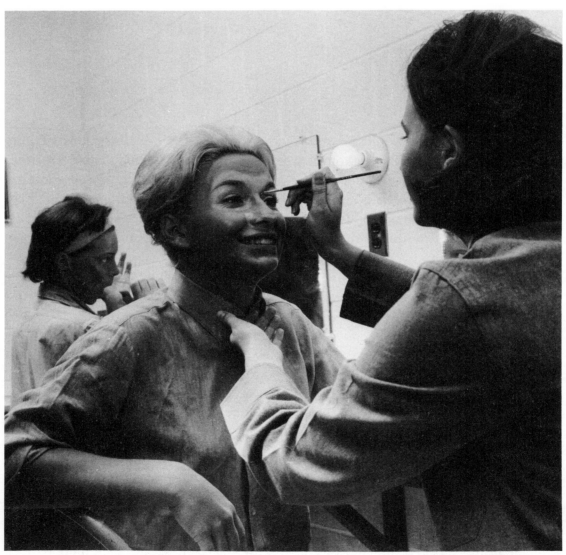

Figure 1 *The joy of theatrical makeup: These students in a makeup course at the Culver Summer Schools, Culver, Indiana, are thoroughly enjoying their newly found craft.*

you are not careful, may find yourself the subject of concern, if not amusement, on the part of your family and friends. You will need two mirrors, a scarf or towel, a flashlight, and as many old photographs of yourself as you can obtain.

First, tie the scarf or towel around your head so that all hair is covered. What is the actual shape of your face? Examine the range of coloring of your skin. Is your hairline uneven, straight, curved, high, or low at the forehead? What are the texture and colors of your eyebrows? The length, denseness, and colors of your eyelashes? (Note the plurals.) What lines have formed or are forming on your face? If they are not readily visible, try frowning, squinting, smiling broadly, and pursing your lips to accentuate them. Study carefully the actual size and shape of your nose and mouth.

Next, using two mirrors, study your profiles with the same intensity. Note the amazing differences between them. No movie star or fashion model would dare be caught short of an instant identification of his or her "good side."

Now, in a dark room, use the flashlight to study the planes of your face. They will not be as readily apparent in ordinary general light. But remember that theatrical lights are generally mounted above and to the sides of the actor, and are more brilliant and concentrated than the lighting to which you are accustomed. In a much larger way than the flashlight, they will tend to exaggerate some features, diminish others, just as your small, concentrated beam

will do. Holding the flashlight in various positions above, around, and beneath your face, note where the highlights and shadows fall: the depth of your eye sockets and the hollows beneath your cheeks, the prominence of your chin, nose, and forehead, the width between your eyes, and so forth.

Finally, make an intense study of your old photographs. Arrange them before you in chronological order, and discover in what ways your face has changed or remained constant since early childhood. On that basis, try to imagine how it will continue to change as you grow older, perhaps using an older relative whom you strongly resemble as a point of reference.

As a test of whether you are sufficiently prepared to study makeup (in particular, as it relates to creating an actual change in your appearance), repeat the first experiment of a self-portrait. Compare it to your first one, and compare them both to your reflection in the mirror. Did you use the same profile or the other one in your second drawing? Are you absolutely *sure* it is your better one?

Having made a thorough examination of your face visually, you should now use the sense of touch for your next step in self-study. Although you will be using pigments to paint when you apply makeup, much as a painter uses pigments on a flat surface, one major difference will be that you must deal with three-dimensional modeling. The makeup artist has the rather complex problem of using color to render realistic a three-dimensional surface, which intense, multidirectional lights tend to make as flat as a blank canvas.

Without a strong natural sense of perspective (which, like mathematical talent, many people do not possess), it is difficult to *see* dimension. Blind people "read" faces with their fingertips, deriving a mental image of a face by feeling its many hills and valleys. To have a better understanding of the dimensional anatomy of your own face, you will need to "see" it with your fingertips.

Beginning at the top, the broad expanse between your hairline and eyebrows, which you refer to as your forehead, is called the *frontal eminence* in scientific anatomical terms.

A thin layer of skin and muscle is tightly stretched over the frontal eminence. With the aging process, as the muscles lose tone and the skin loosens, horizontal wrinkles or furrows form across this area, generally following the outline of the *superciliary arch,* the bow-shaped ledge of bone below the eyebrows, dipping downward just above the nose.

At the outer extremes of the frontal eminence and superciliary arch, you can feel slight depressions in the skull, the *temporal fossae,* or, as they are more commonly known, temples. Any *fossa* is a depression in, or absence of, bone structure. The temporal fossae are not pronounced in youth, but become increasingly obvious with age.

Below the downward dip in the superciliary arch is the *nasal bone,* which study of a skull or a picture of one will show as a very shallow protuberance. The nose is primarily composed of *cartilage,* a tough substance softer and more flexible than bone, which protects and surrounds the *olfactory system,* or sense of smell. The blood vessels of the nose are very near the skin surface, causing quick discoloration in the event of injury or overindulgence.

On either side of the nose are found the *zygomatic arches,* or cheekbones. Although they are not generally regarded as organs of facial expression, their height, prominence, width, and distance from the nose have much to do with the basic shape of the face, and consequently the style in which the hair is worn.

Above the zygomatic arches and below the superciliary arch are found the *orbital fossae,* the round openings that contain the eyeballs. If you run your fingers lightly in a circular motion over your upper and lower eyelids, you can feel the edges of the orbital fossae. If the substance of the eyes and eyelids is naturally receded inward, toward the inside of the skull, and the superciliary arch and edges of the orbital fossae quite prominent in contrast, the makeup artist must consider extensive work in highlighting the orbital area, to accentuate the powers of expression of the eyes. (see Chapter IV).

Immediately below the zygomatic arches are the *infratemporal fossae,* which are responsible for so-called sunken cheeks. Set into these are the *maxilla,* or upper jaw, and the *mandible,* or lower jaw. Dividing the maxilla from the infratemporal fossae are two pronounced lines, the *nasolabial folds.* In old age, these folds sink downward toward the chin, causing what are commonly known as jowls.

On the neck, the structures that will

primarily concern the makeup artist are the *larynx,* or "Adam's apple," and the *mastoid muscles,* which form a "V" on either side of it.

Covering the structures described above is the makeup artist's most immediate concern, the skin. It is composed of two major layers: the *epidermis,* which is the pigmented outer surface we can see and touch, and the *dermis,* directly beneath it, which contains blood and lymphatic vessels, nerves, muscles, glands, and ducts.

The skin is susceptible to many injuries and diseases. This is especially true of the dermis, which can be attacked through the hair and sweat-gland openings of the epidermis.

A final word regarding your skin might be in order here, before you embark upon the transformation of your face through makeup. If you suffer from a skin allergy, or reactions of any kind to commercial cosmetic preparations, you will be well advised to obtain advice from your physician regarding restrictions in the use of makeup, prescriptions for medicated preparations, and so on.

The one *absolute rule* pertaining to the use of makeup is constant cleanliness of the hair and skin. In this regard you dare not be haphazard or half-hearted. You are capable of wreaking irreparable damage to your skin if you do not maintain a perfect regimen of cleaning it, and inasmuch as you cannot discard it yearly for a new one like a snake, you will be stuck for a lifetime with any problems you create!

Chapter II

THE FACE OF THE CHARACTER

*"You've heard me say before that I think the faces
of most American women over thirty are relief maps
of petulant and bewildered unhappiness."*

F. Scott Fitzgerald, in a letter to his daughter.

Assuming you have been cast in a play, musical, opera, or dance drama, you must now virtually get under the skin of the character you are to portray. You will live with and within this person for the period of rehearsals and performances and come to know him *better,* perhaps, than you will ever know yourself!

To proceed in this amazing and exciting task, you will find it necessary to combine the practices of a detective, an artist, a sculptor, a scholar, and a model. In this day and age of sophisticated attendance at all forms of entertainment, it is not enough simply to memorize a specified number of words, haphazardly slap some paint on your face, drape your body in whatever is available, and flail about a stage calling yourself an actor. You must work assiduously at all of the arts and crafts of the theatre, and attempt to achieve the nearest standard to perfection of which you are capable. Acting can be great fun, but to be effective it requires quantities of hard work and attention to detail.

As a detective, you must seek clues about your character, and learn how to interpret them. Naturally, the most obvious clues will be found in the playscript. You must read and reread the script many times outside of regularly scheduled rehearsals in order not to miss a single clue to be found there. Do not limit your reading to your own part; other characters will shed much light on your role through their dialogue, and the playwright often plants splendid characterization hints in stage directions. Shakespeare's plays are illuminated with magnificent descriptions of character, including appearance, and George Bernard Shaw's lengthy prefaces and parenthetical instructions leave virtually no doubt about his people. William Con-

Figure 2 *Director Julien R. Hughes has combined the use of ethnic makeup techniques with masks in this production of* The King and I *at Leuzinger High School, Lawndale, California.*

greve's *The Way of the World* contains some incomparable and hilarious makeup tips for the Restoration comedy of manners.

In the first scene of Act III, Lady Wishfort, seated at her dressing table, addresses her maid, Peg:

Lady Wishfort: I have no more patience. If I have not fretted myself until I am pale again, there's no veracity in me! Fetch me the red—the red, do you hear, sweetheart? An arrant ash-colour, as I am a person!

Look you how this wench stirs! Why dost thou not fetch me a little red? Didst thou not hear me, Mopus?
Peg: The red ratafia does your ladyship mean, or the cherry-brandy?
Lady Wishfort: Ratafia, fool! No, fool. Not the ratafia, fool—grant me patience! I mean the Spanish paper, idiot—complexion, darling. Paint, paint, paint, dost thou understand that, changeling, dangling thy hands like bobbins before thee?
As the scene progresses, Lady Wishfort finally settles on the cherry brandy,

rather than the makeup, to brighten her "pale" face.

The director of the production, and in some cases the designer, will have specific ideas regarding your character and appearance to fit in with an overall concept of the final product.

The truly conscientious actor will seek information beyond the confines of the playscript and the specific production. Libraries are filled with rich sources for the actor-scholar to investigate. Vast quantities of materials exist on past epochs and recent history, including art reproductions and photographs. Biography and autobiography provide excellent insight into fictional characterization.

From research and discussion, the actor-sculptor is ready to adapt his body to the requirements of the role, and to mold and paint his face to fit the characterization.

It is now time to prepare a portrait of the character you will enact. Various actors use various methods: Some actually do a drawing of the face they hope to achieve, sometimes actually painting it in makeup over a self-portrait. Others write elaborate notes to append to their playscripts, literally creating a "pen portrait." Some prefer simply to rely upon a carefully thought-out visual image retained in memory. Only experience can dictate which approach is most feasible for you, but if you are a beginning student of theatre, it might be well to experiment with all of those methods, and eventually devise your own.

You will need to approach your character from several points of view: age, health, temperament, and ethnic background. Too often, the beginning actor will indiscriminately smear his face with an assortment of colors and lines totally unrelated to the qualities of the person he is to enact.

As an example of a pen portrait as mentioned above, note in Figure 3 how an actor's script might contain material vital to his characterization in addition to the playwright's dialogue. The actor playing the small character role of the Soothsayer in Shakespeare's *Antony and Cleopatra* has written in the director's blocking of his movements, and also a few character notes (either his own or those given him by the director), and descriptions of his costume, hand prop, and general makeup. As this actor will also play the part of the Clown near the end of the play, he must make use of a wig and a latex-based beard and mustache, which can be quickly removed, then used again in later performances.

Many actors write many pages of historical and psychological notes throughout their scripts, like footnotes, and even go so far as to detail facial expressions, gestures, and pauses in the delivery of lines, as well as general blocking.

It would be absurd for the young student playing a juvenile such as Romeo, or an ingenue such as Juliet to appear streaked with a network of crow's-feet, jowl lines, and frown wrinkles. By the same token, even older professional actors inevitably find it necessary to resort to considerable use of aging makeup devices in playing King Lear or Mistress Quickly.

65 YRS. OLD — WILY, CLEVER.
LIMPS —

SCENE I.]   **ANTONY AND CLEOPATRA.**   749

Ant. There's beggary in the love that can be reckon'd.
Cleo. I'll set a bourn how far to be belov'd.
Ant. Then must thou needs find out new heaven, new earth.

Enter an Attendant.

Att. News, my good lord, from Rome.
Ant.   Grates me:—the sum.
Cleo. Nay, hear them, Antony:
Fulvia perchance is angry; or, who knows
If the scarce-bearded Cæsar have not sent
His powerful mandate to you, *Do this or this;*
Take in that kingdom and enfranchise that;
Perform't, or else we damn thee.
Ant.   How, my love!
Cleo. Perchance! nay, and most like:—
You must not stay here longer,—your dismission
Is come from Cæsar; therefore hear it, Antony.—
Where's Fulvia's process?—Cæsar's I would say?—both?—   [queen,
Call in the messengers.—As I am Egypt's
Thou blushest, Antony; and that blood of thine
Is Cæsar's-homager: else so thy cheek pays shame   [sengers!
When shrill-tongu'd Fulvia scolds.—The mes-
Ant. Let Rome in Tiber melt, and the wide arch
Of the rang'd empire fall! Here is my space.
Kingdoms are clay: our dungy earth alike
Feeds beast as man: the nobleness of life
Is to do thus; when such a mutual pair   [*Embracing.*
And such a twain can do't, in which I bind,
On pain of punishment, the world to weet
We stand up peerless.
Cleo.   Excellent falsehood!
Why did he marry Fulvia, and not love her?—
I'll seem the fool I am not; Antony
Will be himself.
Ant.   But stirr'd by Cleopatra.—
Now, for the love of Love and her soft hours,
Let's not confound the time with conference harsh:
There's not a minute of our lives should stretch
Without some pleasure now:—what sport to-night?
Cleo. Hear the ambassadors.
Ant.   Fie, wrangling queen!
Whom everything becomes,—to chide, to laugh,
To weep; whose every passion fully strives
To make itself, in thee fair and admir'd!
No messenger; but thine, and all alone,
To-night we'll wander through the streets and note
The qualities of people. Come, my queen;
Last night you did desire it:—speak not to us.
                [*Exeunt* ANT. *and* CLEO., *with their Train.*
Dem. Is Cæsar with Antonius priz'd so slight?
Phi. Sir, sometimes, when he is not Antony,
He comes too short of that great property
Which still should go with Antony.
Dem.   I am full sorry
That he approves the common liar, who
Thus speaks of him at Rome: but I will hope
Of better deeds to-morrow. Rest you happy!
                [*Exeunt.*

SCENE II.—ALEXANDRIA. *Another Room in Cleopatra's Palace.*

Enter CHARMIAN, IRAS, ALEXAS, *and a* Soothsayer.

Char. Lord Alexas, sweet Alexas, most anything Alexas, almost most absolute Alexas, where's the soothsayer that you praised so to the queen? O that I knew this husband, which you say must charge his horns with garlands!
Alex. Soothsayer,—
Sooth. Your will?
Char. Is this the man?—Is't you, sir, that know things?
Sooth. In nature's infinite book of secrecy A little I can read.
Alex. Show him your hand.

Enter ENOBARBUS.

Eno. Bring in the banquet quickly; wine enough
Cleopatra's health to drink.
Char. Good sir, give me good fortune.
Sooth. I make not, but foresee.
Char. Pray, then, forsee me one.   [are.
Sooth. You shall be yet far fairer than you
Char. He means in flesh.
Iras. No, you shall paint when you are old.
Char. Wrinkles forbid!
Alex. Vex not his prescience; be attentive.
Char. Hush!
Sooth. You shall be more beloving than beloved.   [drinking.
Char. I had rather heat my liver with
Alex. Nay, hear him.
Char. Good now, some excellent fortune!
Let me be married to three kings in a forenoon, and widow them all: let me have a child at fifty, to whom Herod of Jewry may do homage: find me to marry me with Octavius Cæsar, and companion me with my mistress.
Sooth. You shall outlive the lady whom you serve.   [than figs.
Char. O excellent! I love long life better
Sooth. You have seen and prov'd a fairer former fortune
Than that which is to approach.
Char. Then belike my children shall have no names:—pr'ythee, how many boys and wenches must I have?
Sooth. If every of your wishes had a womb, And fertile every wish, a million.
Char. Out, fool! I forgive thee for a witch.
Alex. You think none but your sheets are privy to your wishes.
Char. Nay, come, tell Iras hers.
Alex. We'll know all our fortunes.
Eno. Mine, and most of our fortunes, to-night, shall be—drunk to bed.
Iras. There's a palm presages chastity, if nothing else.
Char. Even as the o'erflowing Nilus presageth famine.
Iras. Go, you wild bedfellow, you cannot soothsay.
Char. Nay, if an oily palm be not a fruitful prognostication, I cannot scratch mine ear.— Pr'ythee, tell her but a worky-day fortune.

ENTER UR—STAY BY DRAPES ✗ DR BOW.

(AMUSED)

2 STEPS TO C, LOOK AWAY

D A LITTLE.

TURN, XUL 3 STEPS — BACK TO AUDIENCE, STILL.

1ST COSTUME: LOOSE, HOODED ROBE — OVER CLOWN COSTUME, CARRY STAFF. WHITE WIG — BEARD & MUSTACHE ON LATEX

Figure 3 *Manuscript page from* Antony and Cleopatra *with actor's marginal notes.*

A good actor is a clear thinker, and just as Gilbert and Sullivan's Koko sings of the punishment fitting the crime,[1] so you must use old-fashioned "horse sense" in fitting the face to the character.

Health and temperament are of great importance in preparing a specific makeup and are all too often overlooked. A very elderly person in good health and possessing a jolly nature should no more appear onstage in a sallow makeup with down-turned lines than should a very young person, melancholy and ill, appear all sun-tanned and rouged.

Ethnic background is of prime importance in many theatrical productions, and in creating makeup for a character racially different from yourself, you must perform considerable extra research, observe the racial characteristics with great care, and devote much thought and practice to the creation of the makeup itself.

Among the many tools used in the art of creating fine theatrical makeup are four that you will *always* need, which cannot be found in any makeup kit: logical thought, observation, imagination, and expression.

Logical thought, or "horse sense" has already been taken up to some extent. You should be constantly and purposefully aware of the effect you wish to achieve; *how* to achieve it, and *why* it is the proper one for your role.

Much, if not most, of the how and why of your makeup can be gained through careful and disciplined observation—well beyond reading and research. Everyday living should become your library and your laboratory for makeup—present and future. When you ride a bus, or sit in a park, or wait in a waiting room, instead of burying your nose in a magazine or newspaper, look around you. Study many faces in all kinds of light. Observe the elderly and their various complexions and configurations of lines and wrinkles. Try to figure out what combinations of physical aging and personality have contributed to their facial structures. Look carefully at the myriad shadings of color within any one ethnic group, including your own. (See Figure 2).

The theatre creates its own world of symbols and generalities. A play is an action, or a series of actions in which time and place are condensed, distorted, and human lives are reduced to commonly identifiable basic denominators. An extreme example is the great medieval morality play, *Everyman,* in which human values and traits are distilled in simplified, broad artistic portrayals bearing appropriate names such as "Greed" and "Good Deeds." Such characterization is often most effectively handled with the use of inflexible masks (see Chapter V).

In the ancient Greek theatre, in which every element of the play was gauged for an auditorium on approximately the same scale as a football gridiron, characteristics of the players had to be immediately and easily identified. Thus, the

---

[1] W. S. Gilbert and Arthur Sullivan, *The Mikado* (New York: G. Schirmer, Inc., n.d.)

headdresses attached to the masks had either a high, middle, or low *onkos,* or brow. Gods and kings wore the high onkos, hero-warriors and noblemen the middle, and slaves and concubines the low onkos.

If the nature of the play and the character should lend themselves to a simplified treatment, much imagination and interest can be contributed by the makeup in this respect. Otherwise, the aforementioned subtleties and complexities of psychological expression must be deeply studied.

A word of caution: Observe, but do so with subtlety. It can be most unpleasant to be accused of rude staring!

Imagination is truly the lifeblood of the theatre. It is imagination that writes the play, that creates a world of magic out of commonplaces, that turns you, in the eyes of your audience, into a butcher, baker, candlestick maker, a king, a queen, a beggar, or a beast.

Figures 4, 5, 6, and 7 are all photographs of one actress: Eileen Heckart. Although it is obvious that wonderfully talented makeup artists have contributed much toward creating her visual characterization, this brilliant actress does not *rely* on makeup to convey her roles. Her virtuosity of facial expression is one facet of her talent that makes her great.

Without resorting to cheap "mugging," a talented and disciplined actor can learn, through practice, to convey whatever he wishes his audience to receive. The face is an instrument of fine sensitivity and enormous scope, but whether beautiful or plain, young or old, it is an instrument as rare as the rarest Stradivarius, rendered worthless without many hours of practice, study, *practice.*

Much has been said about the face, because of its expressive powers for the actor. But the good actor uses every means available to him to enact a character. Among the other tools to be considered in connection with makeup, the hands, the feet and legs, and the shoulders have great importance under certain circumstances. We have and will generally consider the neck as an extension of the face.

The hands are extremely suggestive of characterization. They will show whether a person has worked hard and physically, or led a life of leisure; his race, his age, even the state of his health. The difference between long, tapered, well-manicured youthful hands and those that are heavy, muscular, grimed with work, and perhaps freckled with "liver spots," will be readily seen. If the arms and shoulders are bare, they must be made up to greater or lesser extent so that there will not be a "cut-off" line in color or quality (see Figure 33). Certain period plays will demand easily seen beauty patches.

Bare legs and feet also give clues to a character's background. A child who has been playing in a dusty road will require a makeup far removed from a sandaled monk who almost never leaves the dark monastery.

It is sometimes difficult to put all the parts together, and see the whole. An actor must keep many, many parts in mind at all times. If the parts are con-

Figure 4 *Actress Eileen Heckart as she appears in "real life." (Photograph courtesy Ashley Famous Agency)*

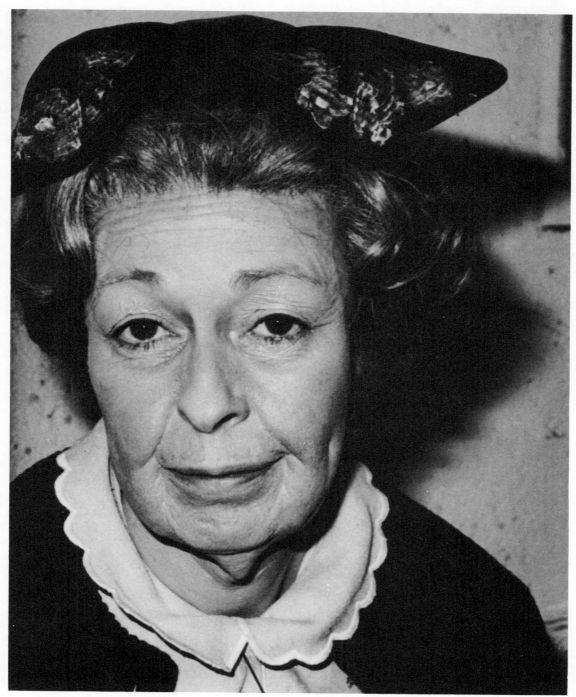

Figure 5 *Miss Heckart is transformed into the lonely old widow of* Save Me a Place at Forest Lawn *with the help of the makeup created by Dick Smith, S.M.A. Note prosthetic constructions. (Photograph courtesy of Dick Smith, S.M.A.)*

Figure 6 and Figure 7   *Eileen Heckart in "psychedelic" makeup (left) for one of her scenes as an off off-Broadway actress in* Secrets *for "CBS Playhouse," and as the actress away from the stage (right). Makeups by Louis Phillippi, S.M.A. (Photograph courtesy of CBS Television)*

sidered well in advance, and, with the director's help, notes are made to avoid forgetfulness in the tension of final rehearsals and performances, the over-all picture the actor presents of himself to the audience will contain no flaws to distract the spectators from the general artistic effect.

Chapter III

THE PREPARATION AND MAINTENANCE
OF THE MAKEUP KIT

"He's a god or a painter, for he makes faces."
Shakespeare, *Love's Labour's Lost,*
Act V, Scene ii.

A makeup kit can be as modest as a few items in a paper bag, or as elaborate as several hundred in a full-sized closet. Professional actors are required to furnish their own makeup in the legitimate theatre, whereas motion picture and television studios provide the highly specialized makeup required by those media, and well-trained professional artists to apply it.[2]

Most theatre students are likely to make use of makeup equipment provided by their schools, possibly augmented by a small collection of personal equipment with which to experiment and practice at home.

Students who must use special non-allergenic makeup should take care to protect their equipment from use by others.

To keep abreast of all the latest developments in makeup would be almost as hopeless as following the new inventions of space-age engineering. As chemistry and medicine become increasingly sophisticated, the field of cosmetics must keep pace as a complex by-product.

Strangely, despite vast progress in the area of theatrical makeup, many of the cosmetics and methods in use today date back thousands of years to the primitive rituals that presaged the "modern" theatre of the ancient Greeks. The word "greasepaint" evokes the mystery, the splendor, and the glamour of the world of the theatre to all those who love it on both sides of the footlights.

In a fascinating article on the history of makeup, M. St. Clare Byrne describes, in considerable detail, the evolution of modern makeup from its origin in crude powdered pigments (often fatal

---

[2] As this book is specifically directed to the *theatre* student, no attempt will be made to deal with the intricacies of motion-picture and television makeup.

to the wearer) to modern preparations. It is amusing to trace the influence of theatrical makeup on public fashion, and vice versa. Miss Byrne says:

Until the introduction of gas and electricity and the invention of grease-paint, make-up in the theatre is the history first and foremost of the use of disguise . . . Even as drama antedates the theatre, so disguise antedates the drama . . .[3]

Early in the history of the theatre, actors discovered that the powders they used tended to streak or even disappear with perspiration. Eventually, they discovered the pigments would adhere to the skin better if applied over a layer of butter, lard, oil, or some pomade, and behold: greasepaint was born. Although nowadays greasepaint is not as highly esteemed as some of the less moist cosmetics (the heat and brilliance of modern electric theatrical lights tend to make it shine, even through powder), it is still very much on the market, and preferred by some.

Many items found in today's makeup kits hark back to the near or distant past in the history of cosmetics: rouge, lining color, eye shadow, and rabbit's-foot brushes. (Who said actors are superstitious?)

The following list of materials and equipment is only a partial one. A full list would seem staggering, not to mention confusing, and probably of little use to the student, as many of the items

on the market today require the knowledge and skills of a well-trained professional makeup artist.

Theatrical makeup is a very expensive item in the budget of any school drama department—and that of any student. It is pointless to suggest even approximate prices of materials here, because by tomorrow, today's prices are as absurd as last year's high fashions. Also, taxes and other considerations cause prices to fluctuate from state to state; even from city to city.

If you are truly interested in seeing the full range of makeup materials from which to choose, it is suggested that you write to the various manufacturers and distributors and ask for their catalogues and price lists. Names and addresses can be obtained from current theatrical periodicals, or by writing to either the American Educational Theatre Association, 815 17th Street N.W., Washington, D.C. 20006, or to the American National Theatre and Academy, 245 West 52nd Street, New York, N.Y. 10019. Your local druggist can also be a valuable source of information, as he has innumerable contacts with a variety of cosmetics wholesale outlets.

Some companies sell prepacked kits of makeup of various sizes and prices. However, they are not particularly recommended. Each person is different, each character is different, each play is different. It would seem wiser to purchase exactly the makeup you need for a specific purpose, thus forming the collection over a long period of time, and without useless excess (and expensive) items. If a new department or a new school were

[3] M. St. Clare Byrne, "Make-up," *The Oxford Companion to the Theatre*, Phyllis Hartnoll, editor (London: Oxford University Press, 1964) pp. 498–509.

to buy a prepacked kit of, for example, costumes, perhaps two each of items suitable for the sixteenth, seventeenth, and nineteenth centuries might arrive, in addition to a Biblical and a Chinese pair. It would probably be quite difficult to find a play to go with the kit. With makeup, it is a little less radical—but not much.

The following items are broken down into basic categories according to use. It is hoped that this list might suggest necessary, and also unnecessary equipment to the teacher and the student.

BASE MAKEUP

The base makeup is just what its name implies: the general, basic coloration for the entire makeup. It is also used for shading and highlighting larger areas.

The oldest and best-known of the bases is greasepaint, which comes in two forms: soft and hard. The hard, or stick, form has a claylike consistency, and requires that the actor apply a softening layer of cold cream or light oil first, in order to soften the paint and make it spreadable.

The greasepaint in tubes or jars has a built-in softener; in the language of the painter, the medium is premixed with the pigment. The soft greasepaint is infinitely easier to use than the stick form.

One great advantage greasepaints have over the dry bases such as pancake makeup is a wider and more subtle spectrum of colors and shades. Another is that they are far less expensive.

On the skin, the paints feel, as their name implies, greasy. An actor who tends to perspire freely will be quite likely to find them unbearable. They are indispensable for use over nose putty, rubber bald wig caps, and other special surfaces that do not readily accept or retain dry or water-soluble makeup.

A wide variety of "cake," dry, or semi-dry makeups is available. They are more comfortable to wear, must be applied with great care, and are frequently difficult to use at first. Once you are accustomed to them, however, you will find that not only do they feel better to the skin, they are also much easier to remove, especially from "tricky" places such as the ears and hairline.

The lightweight "pressed powder" bases made for women's street wear do not hold up well on larger stages, but are of great convenience in small theatres and arenas.

Most of the liquid bases are extremely mild in contact with the skin, and many are medicated preparations for tender skin. The primary shortcoming of the pressed powders and liquid bases is their narrowly limited range of color. Under theatrical lights, a far stronger color value is needed than that required for street or indoor light.

Clown white is the thick, virtually opaque base used by clowns to block out effectively almost all natural expression of the face. It is sticky, viscous, and tends to cause itching of the skin, but is quite harmless. It also sometimes doubles as a highlighting liner or may be used to gray the hair and eyebrows. Caution: It is quite difficult to wash out of the hair, sometimes requiring laundry detergent as a substitute for shampoo.

At the opposite extreme, but with the same effect of flat opacity, is "blackface," or burnt cork. In the seventeenth and eighteenth centuries, burnt pieces of cork mixed in beer or in butter were used by actors portraying Othello and similar parts. Later, it reached a height of popularity with the minstrel shows of the nineteenth and early twentieth centuries.

LINERS

Liners were originally anything from lampblack to simple dirt, applied with the fingers to emphasize the eyes, create strong lines on the face, and so on.

Now, they are generally found in the form of small sticks of firm grease paint or eyebrow pencils. The grease stick liners are applied most effectively with sharp-edged small brushes, or very small water-color brushes, especially the fairly inexpensive ones used for delicate Oriental calligraphy, made with pointed natural bristles in a bamboo handle. Some actors still prefer to use the old-fashioned paper stomps: treated paper rolled tightly into the shape of a pencil stub.

Grease liners range from white through the entire spectrum to black, and some people like to use the red ones for lipstick or rouge, and the blue, green, purple, or brown ones for eyeshadow. "Soft liners" also come in jars or tins.

Eyebrow pencils are made of a soft, waxy crayon pressed into wood, like writing pencils. They should not, however, be sharpened like writing pencils to be most effective. They should be whittled with a single-edged razor blade, so that the crayon forms a flat, slanted wedge (see Figures 9-A, B, C, D), which, when rotated lightly between the fingers, can form either a thick or extremely thin line, or a combination of both. The eyebrow pencil ground down by the wall pencil sharpener gives only a single, round point; not nearly as effective as the wedge-shaped one in creating lines, wrinkles, and other accents.

The primary advantage of grease stick liners over pencils is the wider range of colors and shades. However, pencil lines tend less to unmanageable smearing, and, once the novelty of dealing with the wedge-shaped tip has settled into familiarity, it is easier and quicker to handle.

Liquid liners are available for street wear, although in a limited range of colors. Their containers usually have a brush built into the lid, and in colors of black, brown, and gray, they are quite adequate for stage use.

APPLICATORS

Although small lining brushes have already been discussed, other types are used for other purposes. Larger, soft watercolor brushes of approximately ½″ diameter are excellent for applying rouge. The flat little cotton wafers that generally come packed in the lids of dry rouge tins tend to leave hard, round edges. Those are sometimes appropriate (eccentric old ladies, Commedia dell' Arte characters, clowns), but for a truly natural healthy blush, the soft blend of rouge stroked on with a soft brush is superior.

As mentioned earlier, some actors like to use a large rabbit's paw to apply rouge, or to wipe away excess face powder. Still others like to use puffs of ordinary medicinal cotton. The larger makeup manufacturers sell brushes specifically made

rate the lashes, rather than glue them together in little spikes.

Moistened sponges are used to apply dry, or cake, makeup base. Cotton wads tend to retain too much water, and brushes do not retain enough. Inexpensive sponges made of rubber are adequate, but the ideal sponge for use with

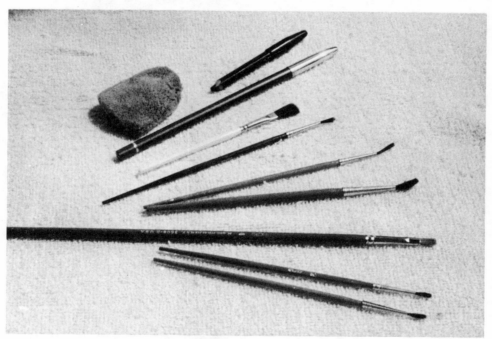

Figure 8 *An assortment of pencils, brushes, and natural sponge used in theatrical makeup. (Photograph by Lynne Anderson)*

for brushing away excess powder. They look very much like fingernail brushes, but instead of being very stiff and pointed, their bristles are soft and rounded. Babies' hairbrushes serve the same purpose.

Professional theatrical mascara brushes are from two to three times the size of those contained in street-wear mascara containers. Because of their size, they are easier to handle with the large cakes of theatrical mascara, and tend to sepa-

cake makeup is the natural (and naturally, more expensive) one. The amount of moisture in the sponge can be regulated more easily, and the raw, uneven edges given to it by nature are ideal for soft-edge blending.

ROUGE

This old cosmetic standby comes in two forms: moist and dry. Moist rouge might either be of a soft grease con-

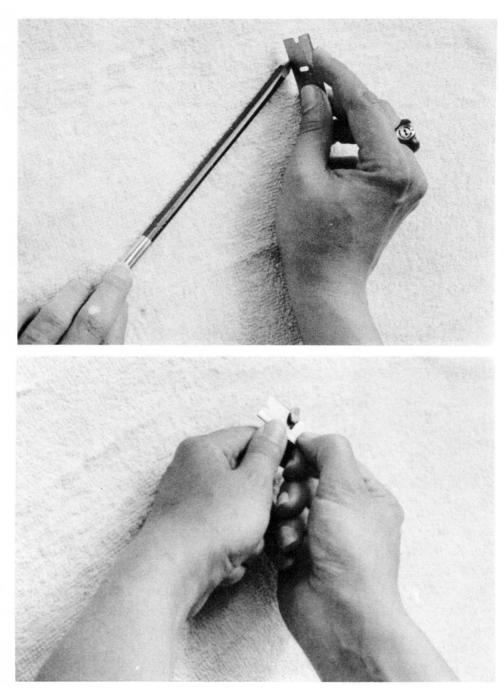

Figures 9-A and 9-B *In Figure 9-A, the tip of the pencil is cut off. In 9-B, the single-edged razor is used to make flat cuts on both sides of the pencil, beginning the wedge.*

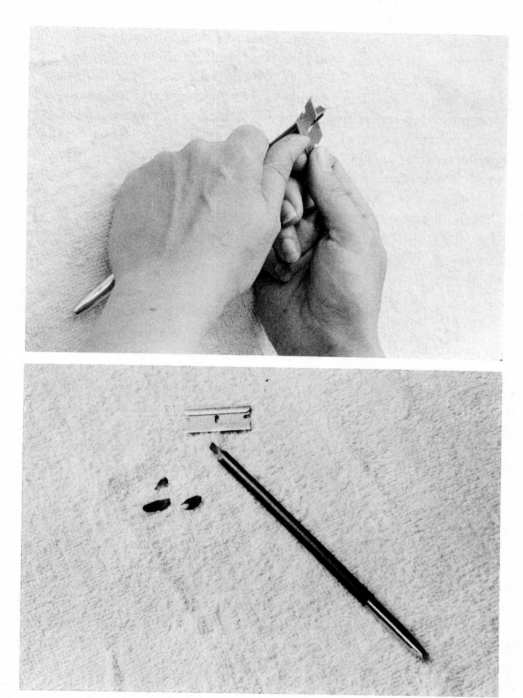

Figures 9-C and 9-D *In Figure 9-C, the edges are trimmed just below the lower edge of the crayon. Figure 9-D: the finished flat, wedge-shaped pencil, ready for lining work. (Photographs by Lynne Anderson)*

sistency, usually sold in jars, or a semi-soft stick liner, which may be ordinary lipstick. It is generally used with grease-paint, although it can be used, with care, over a cake base.

Dry rouge has a consistency similar to that of pressed powder, and is the kind commonly worn for street makeup, as well as the theatre. A light touch and a soft brush are needed for its application.

Both forms of rouge come in a wide range of shades from a light orange hue through vivid primary red into dark bluish or purple-red.

EYE MAKEUP

The eyes being generally regarded as the most expressive area of the face, proper makeup of the eyebrows, lids, lashes, and surrounding skin is of considerable importance. Regular liners are generally used for shading and highlighting. Black, brown, or gray pencils or liners are used to darken or accentuate the brows.

For controlling unruly eyebrows, or blocking out the natural eyebrows entirely in order to paint completely different ones, ordinary hand soap, slightly dampened, is used, stroking it on in the direction of hair growth. To create bushy eyebrows, soft liner is brushed on against the growth of the hair with a mascara brush or toothbrush. The same technique, using clown white, may be used for the aged.

Eye shadow, once generally reserved for use in the theatre, has recently become popular for street wear, and can be found in a variety of colors and forms virtually everywhere. Stick liners may also be used, although some of the more vivid colors might have to be toned down by blending with darker or lighter colors. Soft liners are also frequently used.

Mascara is another material readily available because of its popularity for street wear. Many of the commercial preparations have features, such as eyelash filler to make the lashes look thicker or longer, or are waterproof. Because theatrical mascara does not feature those special qualities, it is generally less expensive. The theatrical preparation usually comes as a simple cake, brown or black, and wrapped in paper. As the applicator brush must be soaked with water in order to use such mascara, a tin box in which some types of cough lozenges are sold is a handy place to keep your mascara cake.

Of the commercial varieties, there is also a cake type that requires water, and generally comes in a plastic or metal case with a small brush. Liquid and paste forms also are sold, with various kinds of brush and corkscrewlike applicators.

A variation on mascara is a waxy preparation called masque, more commonly known as "beading." It is definitely *not* for street wear, and is seldom used on the stage nowadays, although it was highly popular with bygone generations. A woman wearing it was reminiscent of a blackberry bush in a high wind when she blinked. It comes as a hard stick, and must be heated, melted, and applied thickly with a large brush. It is quite difficult to remove.

False eyelashes are the modern substitute for beading to make the lashes appear longer and thicker. They range widely in length, thickness, and, of course, price. Generally, they are a rather expensive item. They are applied with a special adhesive usually packaged with them. Surgical adhesive, readily available in drugstores, also works well. The first time they are used, they should be carefully trimmed by a friend, as they are usually too long, especially at the inside corners of the eyes. They are worn only on the upper eyelid, and should be attached as near to the natural eyelash roots as possible.

POWDER

Face powder is an absolute necessity in any theatre, regardless of how small or intimate it may be. It is essential to "set" a completed makeup with powder, and renew the powder frequently during the performance to keep the face dry (a small container of powder in the wings with a puff and a tissue for brushing away excess is useful).

Even if a "straight" or light street makeup, or no makeup at all is worn, as, for example, in intimate arena playing, or readers' theatre, a light dusting of powder should nevertheless be worn to keep the face dry and unshiny.

Theatrical powder should be used, if possible. It is less expensive than powders made for street use, and inasmuch as large quantities of it must be used for the stage, the rather large containers in which it comes packed, with proportionately large puffs, can be very convenient.

Powder for the theatre comes in a wide variety of colors and shades, to be used with the many special colors of base and lining makeup. For general use, there is also a transparent, neutral shade that does not alter the basic color of the makeup.

When powder is applied to theatrical makeup, it should not be stroked or patted onto the face as is the case with street makeup. The puff should be heavily loaded with powder, then pressed flat against the skin, in order not to smear lines. It should be allowed to "set" for a few moments, then the excess brushed away lightly with the powder brush. A word to the wise: Brush from the center outward to the edge of the face, to avoid getting powder in the nose and eyes.

A new compound, only recently made for the commercial makeup market, might be used as a substitute for powder. It is a cosmetic fixative, not unlike the fixative artists use on paintings of chalk or charcoal to "set" the pigment so that it will not smear or flake away. Contained in an aerosol can, it is sprayed onto the completed makeup from a distance of about twelve inches. The user must, of course, be careful to close the eyes, and not use an excess of the material.

Even if the spray cosmetic "set" is used, powder will probably be required for use backstage to absorb and dry the shiny perspiration that accumulates during actual performance.

HAIR MATERIALS

The most commonly used and well-known theatrical hair preparation is crêpe hair. Although other types of hair may be used in the theatre, they are generally more expensive, in some cases quite difficult to prepare and use, and not always as effective. Among them are mohair, other types of animal hair, human hair, and blends of synthetic hair.

Crêpe hair comes packed in strips of varying lengths, tightly braided. When the hair is unbraided, it is quite kinky, and somewhat matted. In some cases, the curliness is desirable, in which case you simply take the matting out with a wide-toothed comb.

If straight hair is preferable, the hair should be soaked in lukewarm water for a few minutes after unbraiding, then stretched and allowed to dry. It can be stretched between chair or table legs by tying the ends of the strip with string, or between lines, anchored by clothes pegs. Another way of straightening it is to iron it beneath a wet cloth, being sure to keep the iron at a low heat.

Crêpe hair is generally used for making mustaches, beards, and sideburns, although it can also be utilized for making simple wigs on a rubber swimming cap trimmed down to form a proper hairline.

The hair is attached to the skin or rubber cap with spirit gum, liquid latex, or surgical adhesive. The latex is also useful for making a reusable base for a beard or mustache. For dressing certain kinds of beards and mustaches, such as the severely pointed Van Dyke beard or handlebar mustache, mustache wax should be purchased, or a heavy, thick hair pomade.

Several preparations may be used for altering the appearance of your own hair. Probably the most convenient is an aerosol hair spray. It is clear, does not give the greasy appearance of pomade, and if sprayed on fairly heavily, can be very effective in altering the shape and dressing of your own hair; for example, changing or obliterating a part. Most hair tonics and dressings are quite good, again provided they do not appear too shiny or greasy.

On certain characters, of course, such an effect might be desirable, such as the villain in a nineteenth century "mellerdrammer." Also, if the hair has a strong natural curl in it, and some straightening is desirable, a heavy pomade is effective, and will not damage the hair as might some of the strong chemical hair straighteners in use.

It is frequently necessary to change the color of the hair, and several preparations may be used to do so. Hair sprays are made in a variety of colors, including silver and frosty white for graying effects. Also made for the purpose of aging the hair is liquid white mascara.

Time was when cornstarch or talcum powder was brushed into the hair to gray it. The practice can lead to unintentional comedy if, in a scene of violent action, a cloud of white powder puffs up from the actor's head. A very dangerous practice for coloring the hair, and one in which you should never indulge, is to use aluminum or gold bronzing powder combed into the hair. The metallic powder might work its way into a tiny scratch or scalp irritation and cause eventual blood poisoning. If you wish a metallic sheen on the hair, only commercially prepared sprays should be used.

It is unlikely that a theatre student would need to take so radical a step as to alter the color of the hair by means of dyeing, but if such a step is taken, it should always be performed by an experienced beautician. Disastrous results can occur both in terms of the appearance and the health of the hair if dyes fall into inexperienced hands.

Some color rinses and shampoos on the market are advertised as not leaving permanent color in the hair. However, several shampoos are generally required before all traces of the coloring element are removed. In addition, many of the rinses tend to rub off easily, staining clothing, pillowcases, etc.

A rather messy, and possibly dangerous, method of darkening the hair is to rub it with carbon paper. Another foolishly amateur way of coloring the hair, and equally as dangerous as the use of bronzing powder, is to comb shoe polish into the hair.

Sometimes a rather radical period or fantasy style of hair is required. In such a case, a wig, hairpiece, or fall might be used. They can be rented quite easily, and at reasonable rates or, if you are particularly ambitious, you can make one. Professional wig companies have fantastically wide varieties of wigs and hairpieces from which to choose; they are sturdily and attractively made, and sent to you properly dressed. Company catalogues generally include instructions for measuring the head and face for wigs and beards (facial hair on special bases can be rented or purchased, too), and such measurements should be made with great care.

Hairpieces, wigs, and falls are made of an assortment of materials, the best being real human hair. They are mounted on sturdy cloth and/or elasticized bases, edged with a virtually invisible lightweight bobbinette called the "lace." The lace, glued to the forehead and in front of the ears with spirit gum, serves to hold the wig properly in place, even in the most violent stage action. Falls are a little less reliable, as one must depend upon bobby pins and elastic to secure them to the head.

Although wigs and hairpieces are readily available for purchase on the public market, great caution should be exercised in utilizing such hair in the theatre. Most of the comparatively inexpensive ones are made of chemical fibers that look realistic enough in daylight or ordinary room light, but can be disastrous under colored light.

Just as the chemical processes involved in photography can wreak havoc for the photographer not accustomed to the effects of color filters on lighting instruments, so the wigs of man-made fibers can create problems. If the synthetics are tested under filtered light early enough in the rehearsal period to assure the actor there will be no problem in wearing the wig, all is well. But if he appears in a wig necessary for the characterization at a dress rehearsal, and the light changes its color, he, the wig, and the production are in serious trouble.

Figure 10 *King Richard in* Richard III *at Memphis State University, Memphis, Tennessee, showing careful attention to wig, beard, and mustache dressing.*

Figure 11 *Memphis State University students appearing in* The School for Wives *demonstrate a variety of period wigs.*

Blue, blue-green, and some green light medium filters, or "gels," are the worst offenders in terms of changing hair color. Unfortunately, those are the very colors so often used for moonlight or other night scenes, and the blues in particular are generally used as blending colors.

Brunette and black synthetic hair turns to a deep, blood red; medium brown and auburn turn bright orange, and blond or gray turn psychedelic pink. If an effect of hair changing color at night is required by the script of the play, by all means utilize these peculiar properties of the synthetic fibers. If not, forewarned is forearmed!

The aforementioned rubber swimming cap can be effective as a bald, or partially bald wig, and with crêpe hair, knitting yarn, embroidery silk, or other ma-

Figure 12 *Wig on styrofoam wig-block, which keeps it clean and ready for wear onstage.*

terials, can be made into amusing fantasy wigs. In the areas of stylized theatre, fantasy, and farce, the imagination and the materials it demands can run riot.

In his excellent book *Stage Makeup,* Richard Corson provides explicit illustrated instructions on how to make professional wigs. It would not be recommended that the student undertake such a procedure without a reasonably thorough acquaintance with the structure and handling of rented or purchased wigs. A modest experiment should first be attempted: perhaps a small mustache; then if you find you have the patience and skill to perform this "ventilating" operation, you might wish to try a wig. (Patience is mentioned because the hair must be drawn through the base and knotted in tiny individual tufts of a few hairs each.)[4]

A requisite accessory to wigs and hairpieces is a wig block. The best kind to have is one made of cloth-covered cork with a weighted bottom. They are quite expensive, however, and the more readily available and inexpensive styrofoam blocks are suitable. The block is contoured to the shape and size of the head, and the wig is fastened to it with long corsage pins for dressing (see Figure 12).

A wig should be dressed after every performance and shampooed frequently. It should be brushed and combed just like your own hair and set in curlers, hairpins, or bobby pins, depending upon the hair style desired. Regular hair sprays and dressings may be used on wigs, both

[4] Richard Corson, *Stage Makeup* (New York: Appleton-Century-Crofts, 1967), pp. 215–24.

in setting them and adjusting the style once it is being worn.

Wigs should be shampooed with laundry or dish detergent, thoroughly rinsed, and allowed to dry at room temperature on a wig block. The lace should be cleaned after each wearing with acetone to clear it of spirit gum and makeup.

Sometimes, if the hair is badly matted, a brush made with wire bristles (a dog brush) proves more effective in clearing the matting than an ordinary brush or comb.

To preserve the styling of a wig, particularly a long-haired, elaborate one, the use of a fine, lightweight hairnet the color of the wig is recommended. Depending upon the wig style, the hairnet can even be left on the wig when worn onstage.

Between uses, wigs should be kept on a form (a wig block, or at least a shaping of wadded-up tissue paper) and stored in plastic bags or individual cardboard boxes.

SPECIAL MATERIALS

Just about anything in the world can become makeup material in the hands of an imaginative actor or makeup artist, provided it will not harm the skin or affect the health of the actor in any way. The enormously talented artist Dick Smith, S.M.A., who created Miss Heckart's makeup in Figure 5, Hal Holbrook's makeup for *Mark Twain Tonight,* and many other extraordinary makeups for stage, film, and television, is a case in point. In his wonderfully amusing and instructive volume, *Do-It-Yourself Mon-*

ster Make-up Handbook, he calls for such ingredients as corn syrup, flour, pipe cleaners, Ping-Pong balls (cut in half and painted, they make fabulous monster eyeballs), paper towels, and candy chewing wax! [5]

Necessity being the mother of invention, you might well be the creator of a revolutionary new makeup technique while coping with a special makeup problem.

A few suggestions in the area of special makeup equipment follow; most are commercial or professional theatrical items.

Over a period of several centuries, incidents have been reported of fatal makeup. Actors covering, or almost covering, their entire bodies with "body paint" of various sorts (generally gilt or lead pigment) in order to represent statues, angels, and the like, have perished as a result of the inability of their pores to function—a strange and horrible form of suffocation.

Nowadays, makeup preparations are manufactured in a good range of colors, including gold and silver, which may be used on exposed areas of the body without fear of harm. They are liquids, sold in pint and quart bottles, and match, or closely approximate, all colors of base facial makeup.

The bottle of body makeup must be thoroughly shaken, then can be applied either like hand lotion from the palms, or with a sponge.

For those whose teeth are less than

---

[5] Dick Smith, *Do-It-Yourself Monster Make-up Handbook* (New York: Warren Publishing Co., 1965), 98 pp.

Figure 13 *In a* Wizard of Oz *production at Principia Upper School, St. Louis, Missouri, the "Cowardly Lion" has an imaginative blending of costume and makeup to create a fantasy-animal character.*

perfect in shape and color, or who have light-reflecting fillings in the front of the mouth, preparations are made to give you a real billboard smile (or almost). Tooth enamels are made in several shades, and to block out teeth your character has lost, or to shorten long teeth, there is a black tooth wax. Among the shades of available enamel are yellowish and brownish ones that can be used if your characterization calls for dark, deteriorating teeth.

Another form of "remedial" makeup is found in the various commercial preparations, available at all drugstores and notion shops, for covering skin blemishes. The preparations come in liquid, soft grease, and cake forms, and are used under the base makeup. Be sure not to use one of the greasier types underneath a dry pancake base. Although skin blemishes are not likely to be detected by the audience in large proscenium auditoriums, such occupational hazards as cuts and black eyes, as well as ordinary blemishes, can be effectively masked in intimate theatres and arena-style productions with such preparations.

Fishskin, applied with spirit gum, is useful for drawing out the corners of Occidental eyes to make them look Oriental; also for drawing down the lower eyelid to form a pouch beneath the eye. Efficient substitutes are adhesive tape and lightweight silk or net, if you cover them with sufficient makeup to mask the edges.

Blood on the stage, contrary to popular belief, is not catsup. If you stop to think about it, catsup does not really resemble blood. Commercial preparations of stage blood are sold in pint bottles, or you can make it yourself. Dry pigment, such as the kind used to paint theatrical scenery when mixed with glue size, can be mixed with glycerine, which may be purchased at any drugstore. One of the darker lake red colors or turkey red work best.

Neither the commercially prepared nor the "homemade" blood above can be used in or near the mouth. In such cases, Dick Smith's recipe is probably best:

Stir some flour or white frosting mix into some clear [corn syrup] until it looks quite cloudy. Then mix in enough . . . red food color to get a good blood color. If the mixture turns out too thick, add a little water; if too pink, add more red; if too transparent, add more flour.[6]

Beauty patches, a virtual necessity for late seventeenth- and early eighteenth-century plays, can be made from black or colored bits of paper or cloth and attached to the skin with spirit gum or surgical adhesive. Although it might be easier simply to paint on beauty marks with liner or pencil, it is dangerous and unwise. If the play includes a love scene for your character, it is highly embarrassing to draw away from your *vis-à-vis* following a passionate embrace to find your beauty patch imprinted on his or her face. The same holds true for penciled mustaches and sideburns.

Plastic or paste jewels are most effective as rather special beauty marks, as are costumers' sequins. They, too, are applied with spirit gum or surgical ad-

[6] *Ibid.*, p. 56.

hesive. In certain Oriental societies, particularly in India, jewels are embedded in the skin of infants to denote ranks of royalty. The noble Indian woman's forehead ruby can be more effectively represented by a costume jewelry red stone than by moist rouge, but check out your research on this; certain lower-caste Indian women *do* wear rouge spots.

Sequins can also be most attractive sprinkled in the hair, anchored with hair spray. They can also create a fantastic effect just underneath the eyebrows (see Figure 6). They are also attractive sprinkled along the tops of the shoulders and down the arms with *décolleté* gowns. ("Sprinkled" is a euphemism; they must be carefully placed with adhesive.)

Prosthesis is a medical term meaning, essentially, any false anatomical part. Because it has become, over the years, a very important part of the art of makeup, the nature and use of prosthetic makeup is included here.

Probably the oldest of the prosthetic makeup products is nose putty. It is a flesh-colored, claylike substance that one "works" in much the same way as modeling clay. It comes in stick form, and must be rubbed and kneaded in the palms of the hands to make it pliable enough for use.

Nose putty is built up, layer by layer, to form the appearance of extra tissue on the top of the nose, on the chin, to form jowls, more prominent cheekbones, and such.

It must be spun in the palms until it forms a "worm," then, while it is still warm and pliable, laid onto the area to be built up. When the buildup has been completed, the edges must be smoothed out, so that there is not a sharp, visible edge between the skin and the prosthetic device. If it sticks to the hands, it can be lubricated with cold cream or mineral oil. If it becomes too soft on the face, too pliable to hold the shape intended for it, it can be hardened by a sprinkling of cold water.

A material used in about the same way, building gradually small pieces at a time, but that is easier to use and more reliable, has the unfortunate name of mortician's wax. Unlike nose putty, it does require the use of an adhesive such as spirit gum, but in handling it, much the same method is used. It is made in two consistencies under the theatrical name of derma wax: soft and firm. Soft wax is easier to use and moves with the movements of the facial muscles more freely.

Mortician's wax must receive a sealing coat of flexible collodion after the form has been made and blended on the face. The coat prepares it to receive makeup to blend it with the rest of the face. Nose putty does not require such a coat, as long as greasepaint is used to color it.

Collodion is available in drugstores, but because there are two distinct types, you should know which is used for what purpose, and the name. Flexible collodion is a clear, transparent liquid that dries and hardens to a plasticlike surface that will take and retain makeup. Used in combination with surgical cotton, prosthetic pieces can be built, but it is a long, tedious, and often unsuccessful process.

Nonflexible collodion is also a clear, transparent liquid. However, its function is to draw the skin when applied: It causes the skin to pucker and wrinkle and is used primarily for scars and minor deformities. Unfortunately, its effect is so subtle that it is virtually useless for larger theatres.

Figure 14 *A young actor wears a prosthetic putty nose in the Honolulu, Hawaii, Theatre for Youth production of* Young Abe Lincoln. *Note the deep shading in the hollows of the cheeks to simulate Lincoln's gaunt features.*

REMOVAL AND CLEANING MATERIALS

As was pointed out in Chapter I, cleanliness in makeup matters is next to godliness, if not more. Many materials may be used for the removal of makeup, not the least of which is old-fashioned soap and water. *Every* makeup kit should contain a bar of soap.

Cold cream is an old standby. Many forms and brands are found on the public and theatrical markets, including an unperfumed one for men. Some actors prefer mineral oil—again, because it is odorless; also, it is easy to obtain. For people and theatre groups on very tight budgets, commercial frying fats work as well as cold cream. It is not necessary to resort to lard or butter; if the can of shortening is covered with plain paper, no one will know that the actor is using the same thing to remove his makeup that his mother uses to fry chicken.

Acetone is an excellent solvent for all kinds of paint: it will remove scene paint and glue from the hands when all else fails; it is a necessity for the removal of accumulated spirit gum and makeup from wig laces and prepared hairpieces; it harmlessly and painlessly removes spirit gum, collodion, and prosthetic remnants (not to mention nail enamel, of which acetone is the base).

Nose putty and mortician's wax can be easily removed (except for a thin film) by running a piece of common sewing thread under the prosthetic piece.

Isopropyl or rubbing alcohol is a good second best to acetone as a cleaning solvent. If acetone is not available, alcohol will generally suffice, and because of hazards in the theatre, it is a good chemical to have on hand as a first-aid supply.

Depending upon your personal preferences, you may wish to maintain your own supply of special cleansing agents. *Pumice* is hard, volcanic lava that is frequently used to remove makeup or dirt deeply ground into the skin surface. In a powdered form, it is frequently combined with soap, cream, or oil, and can be invaluable in removing such cosmetics as the so-called "indelible" lipsticks.

Many people like to use the small paper towels that are available already impregnated with a cleansing agent. They are cooling, cleansing, and have a pleasant, though not perfumed, odor.

It may also be advisable to use blemish medication and astringents following the removal of makeup. Astringents, including after-shave lotions, cut grease and oil, and evaporate perspiration from the skin surface.

If special hair makeup is required by the character, and you prefer to wash it out before leaving the theatre, shampoo, hair rinse, and a hair dryer will be added to your supplies.

One item *every* actor should carry with him is a nail file. Grease, makeup, and ordinary theatrical backstage dirt accumulate alarmingly under the fingernails.

It is a good idea to keep on hand a box or bottle of laundry or dish detergent. It is useful for washing out hosiery, tights, gloves, and wigs. Sometimes even your own hair.

Cotton, facial tissues, and toilet tissues are all useful for removing makeup and removal compounds. It is generally a point of pride that the student provides his own tissues, even if all other makeup and removal equipment is furnished by the school. Soap, a washcloth, and towel are also the personal responsibility of the individual, for obvious sanitary reasons.

Container

A facetious reference was made to a paper bag as a makeup kit, and it was definitely facetious. The fact of the matter is, the container for even a small collection of makeup items should be metal, or at least flame-resistant. Certain elements of theatrical makeup are highly flammable, and the theatre is a place in which flame is a synonym for fear. Very often, makeup is left near the hot light bulbs that often surround makeup mirrors. Their heat is all that is needed to set a paper or cardboard container afire.

Hardware stores have a good selection of toolboxes or fishing tackle boxes. Because of the range in sizes, they can be suitable for either personal or group makeup kits. In larger departments, metal-shelved closets or large metal file cabinets function well.

Whether for personal or general use, any makeup kit needs mirrors. Not just one; several are preferred: at least two. It may be all very well to say smugly you will never go out on tour, but you might be amazed at where you might find yourself someday—and without a mirror! It is useful to have two mirrors regardless of your theatre setup, because one often needs rear-view and profile viewing.

The makeup kit is a good place to keep first-aid equipment: nothing to challenge a doctor, but a small, basic kit, containing at least antiseptic, Band-aids, adhesive, cotton, aspirin, eyewash, and a petroleum jelly. You will also be amazed at how often the first-aid supplies are enlisted for makeup.

If you are primarily interested in a personal collection of makeup, certain items, as personal as any you will find in your personal luggage, must be included (and once your mind is made up to become an actor, your makeup automatically becomes a part of your luggage).

The makeup kit is a good place to keep such items as a washcloth and towel, a comb and brush, spare shoes, stockings, and underwear, deodorant, talcum powder, a toothbrush and paste, scissors, a nail file, thread (preferably a small sewing kit), a razor and single-edge blades.

Makeup is expensive, as has been pointed out, and it can be a real necessity, and most personal. For that reason, it is strongly suggested that there be a good, strong lock on the makeup kit or closet.

The materials contained in the makeup kit should be regularly cleaned, and should be packed neatly in their separate categories. You would not care to use a sponge or brush caked with makeup used by someone else six months ago, would you? Responsibility for an institutional kit seems to be a matter of personal conscience. As to the personal kit: It is yours, and if you care to deal with your own sloppiness and lack of organization, that is *your* problem, no one else's.

THE DRESSING ROOM

Most theatres are built with dressing rooms near the stage, but some are not. You might find yourself in a makeshift situation, such as in a large room "adapted" as an arena-style theatre. In a gymnasium-turned-theatre, locker rooms will probably be used. No matter where a theatrical troupe may find itself,

a place must be provided for changing costumes and applying makeup.

Ideally, there should be a *minimum* of two dressing rooms: one for men, one for women. They should be large enough to accommodate the large cast of a musical comedy, and if one is to be larger than the other, it should probably be the men's, as most casts contain more men than women.

If smaller, individual rooms are provided, there should still be at least two larger rooms for a chorus and/or dance corps. Sanitary lavatory and toilet facilities should also be provided, and, if possible, showers. Dressing rooms should also have adequate ventilation facilities.

All too often, in the planning of theatres, elaborate plumbing installations are provided for the public areas: lobbies, office and classroom areas, and near exits. Sometimes, running water and drainage are provided for scenery and wardrobe shops, but it would amaze you how often dressing rooms, if included at all, contain nothing more than a single washing sink.

Actors, being actors, learn to cope with just about everything. But if you are ever in a position to have something to say about the planning and construction of a theatre, make your voice heard when it comes to dressing rooms.

Ventilation is an item that may need some clarification. Ventilation does *not* mean a window that can be opened, although under many circumstances that is all you will find. Ideally it should consist of an exhaust fan or system of some kind, because overheated actors certainly will not care to open a window in a cold climate in the dead of winter; nor will they dare open a window in a dirty, sooty location. A circulating air system is perfect, although a simple exhaust fan is very good.

Many of the chemicals used in makeup are volatile and create a real hazard when inhaled. Others, although not necessarily dangerous, are evil-smelling in the extreme. Also, natural body, clothing, and shoe odors are not pleasant to work in. The preponderant aerosol-can products demand ventilation for their use.

Because of the fire hazard of makeup chemicals discussed earlier, each dressing room should also contain easily operated, up-to-date fire extinguishers, automatic sprinkling systems, or a combination of both.

The importance of lighting in dressing rooms cannot be exaggerated. It should create, as much as possible, the same lighting environment to be found on the stage. Lights should be high-intensity incandescent bulbs (fluorescent lighting, although cheaper and cooler, distorts color). If possible, the lights should surround the makeup mirrors, and, for optimum effect, have devices to hold samples of color media, such as gel or glass, in the colors to be used in the actual production.

Mirrors are, of course, an absolute necessity. There can never be too many mirrors in a theatre. It is best if each actor has an individual mirror; whatever the situation, as many mirrors as possible should be provided. They can be mounted either on tables or on walls, with ledges or shelves beneath them for use as makeup tables. Every theatre needs *at least* one full-length mirror, so that the actor can get the full effect of costume, makeup, wig: a view of himself as the audience will see him, head to toe.

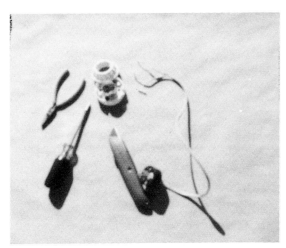

Figure 15 *Materials needed for wiring light socket. Male plug already wired; the socket has been unscrewed and is ready to be attached to other end of cord.*

Real theatrical mirrors, with the necessary lights attached, can be made very easily and quite inexpensively. Materials required are a mirror, which might be any simple old looking glass from an attic or thrift shop, provided it has a wooden or composition-board frame; sockets, wood screws, lengths of common household electrical cord, male plugs, and a knife, screw-driver, a pair of pliers, electrical tape, and light bulbs.

In selecting, begging, borrowing, or buying a mirror, aside from the necessity for a wood frame, the main requisite you should keep in mind is that it be made of clear, unbroken glass, has few or no flaws in its silver backing, and has been thoroughly cleaned.

The sockets, wire, and plugs can be obtained from any hardware store or shop dealing in varieties of household electrical appliances. The socket may be porcelain, Bakelite, or rubber, and it might be in either one or two pieces, the latter providing a covering for the electrical contacts. The socket used in the illustrations is a porcelain two-piece socket. Whichever kind is used, it must be a receptacle for regular-sized light bulbs, and must have a flat surface with two holes so that it can be screwed to the mirror frame.

Using the cutting part of the pliers, clip a piece a few inches longer than the length you wish the cord to be from the length of household electrical cord. In the center of the cord is a slight indentation. If the cord on each side of it is lightly pulled, two pieces of wire will separate. Run the knife lightly around the rubber or plastic covering the copper wire, then remove the covering by pulling it off the end. This is called "stripping" the wire. Roll the copper wire between your thumb and finger to make a solid copper contact ending of the wire. The procedure must be followed at both ends of the cord.

String one end of the split cord through the center opening of the plug (be sure it is a male plug: in other words, the pronged plug that fits into the wall receptacle). Just to the side of each prong of the plug you will find a screw; these screws, which should be loosened to receive the loop of copper wire, are the electrical contacts. Forming a simple loop of copper, wrap it in a clockwise direction around the screw in such a way that when the screw is tightened, none of the copper wires touches any metal part of the plug

except the body and head of the screw itself. Thus, between the prongs of the plug the cord is split, and each of the two terminal screws holds down a loop of stripped copper wire. For perfect safety, a piece of cardboard or plastic (often furnished with the plug) should be slipped over the prongs of the plug to cover the exposed terminals. Otherwise, small pieces of electrician's tape may be used to cover the screw heads.

In Figure (15) the plug has been wired, and the other end of the cord is stripped and ready to be wired onto the socket. The top, or covering portion of the socket has been removed, and the terminal screws may be seen on either side of the round opening that will contain the light bulb. The stripped wire is looped around the screws in exactly the same way as was done on the plug. On certain other types of socket, the screws are exposed on either side of the outside, and should be covered with tape.

In Figure (16) the bottom part of

Figure 16 *Wired socket is attached to frame of mirror with wood screws.*

the socket has been wired and has been positioned on the wooden frame of the mirror. It is now attached with ordinary wood screws driven through the holes in the sides of the socket and approximately one-half to three-quarters of the depth of the frame. Following this, the top half of the socket is screwed onto the bottom half, and a light bulb inserted into the socket opening (Figure 17).

Figure 17 *Completed makeup mirror.*

As many or as few lights as desirable may be attached to the frame of a mirror in this way, and for extra protection, chicken-fence wire may be attached over the entire unit (including the bulb) with electrical tape. This will prevent costume fabrics and makeup equipment from burning on the bulb, and should the light bulb blow out and explode, it will protect any people nearby from flying glass.

Removing the light bulbs and carefully packing them, this unit becomes readily portable if you are traveling with a production which might play in theatres not equipped with this type of mirror. The mirror can be attached to a wall or makeup table for permanent use in your own theatre dressing room, or, with the help of a metal shop-worker, you may want to hinge it and attach it to your makeup case or cabinet.

Because electrical cord is very cheap, and frustration can be expensive, be sure to allow more than enough cord on your light rigging. It is better to have too much than too little.

The makeup table or tables should be of comfortable height for the actors who sit at them and should contain enough surface space to accommodate the equipment necessary for a full makeup, including a wig block. In ideal circumstances, the tables will also have shelf and/or drawer space for additional equipment, preferably with locks for personal valuables.

The dressing rooms should also contain adequately ventilated spaces for the hanging of costumes and street clothing, as well as shelves for shoes, gloves, hats, and such.

If the school or other producing organization maintains a collection of makeup, it should be kept in a metal container (a standing metal wardrobe with adjustable shelves is ideal) that can be locked. If possible, two should be provided: one for the men's dressing room or dressing-room area, and one for the women's. One person should be made responsible for keeping the makeup clean, neat, and in plentiful

Figure 18.

DATE: _____

INVENTORY OF MAKEUP

NAME, COLOR, DESCRIPTION, BRAND	NUMBER ON HAND	NUMBER TO ORDER
Foundation: Grease		
FACTOR #4½	2	2
FACTOR #7A	1	4
LEICHNER #8A	1	8
LEICHNER DARK MAUVE	1	8
STEIN #17	1	8
STEIN #3½	3	2
Foundation: Dry or Cake		
MEHRON #27A	1	3
FACTOR #5N PANCAKE	3	1
FACTOR #2N PANSTIK	1	1
STEIN TAN BLUSH 2	4	0
STEIN CREAM A	2	3
Rouge: Moist		
STEIN #14	1	3
FACTOR DARK CINECOLOR	1	0
MEHRON #11	2	0
Rouge: Dry		
MEHRON #GERANIUM	1	2
FACTOR RASPBERRY	4	2
FACTOR BLONDEEN	1	0
STEIN #14	1	3
STEIN #18	2	0
Liners		
FACTOR #10	2	0
LEICHNER #22	2	2
STEIN #17	1	4
STEIN #21	2	0
Pencils: Black	4	4
Pencils: Brown	6	0
Pencils: Gray	4	0
Pencils: Other		
MAROON	0	4
WHITE	1	1
Powder		
STEIN NEUTRAL	6	2
FACTOR #6	2	0
Powder Puffs	4	6
Powder Brushes	6	0
Lining Brushes and stomps		
FINE BRUSHES (WATERCOLOR)	25	0
CHINESE "	2	4
LARGE ROUGE BRUSHES	4	0
Mascara and Masque		
BLACK	4	0
BROWN	4	0
BLUE	1	0

Figure 18 (Continued)

Mascara Brushes	6	2
False Eyelashes	4 PRS.	0
Eyelash Adhesive	2 TUBES	0
Surgical Adhesive	1 TUBE	4 TUBES
Liquid Latex	2 BOTTLE	0
Nose Putty	4 STICKS	0
Derma Wax	2 TINS	0
Spirit Gum	4 BOTTLE	2 BOTTLES
Adhesive and Gum Brushes	10	8
Collodion: Flexible	1 BOTTLE	0
Collodion: Inflexible	1 BOTTLE	0
Isopropyl Alcohol	0	4 BOTTLES
Acetone	2 GAL.	0
Crêpe Hair BLACK	1 YD.	1 YD.
LT. BRN.	½ YD.	1 YD.
DK. GRAY	2 YDS.	0
WHITE	0	1 YD.
Other Hair		
BLACK DYNEL	1 HANK	0
WHITE MOHAIR	0	1 HANK
Scissors	2 PRS.	4 PRS.
Hair Whitener	1 BOTTLE	3 BOTTLES
Hair Spray and Dressing		
GOLD SPRAY	2 CANS	0
BLACK "	0	1 CAN
POMMADE HONGROISE (MUSTACHE WAX)	1	0
Hairpins and Combs	∝	∝
Clown White	3 TINS	0
Tooth Wax and Enamel	∝	∝
Makeup Remover		
COLD CREAM	4 LG. TINS	2 TINS
MINERAL OIL	2 BOTTLE	0
TISSUES	1 BOX	12 BOXES
Absorbent Cotton	1 BOX	0
Razor Blades	2 PKGS.	2 PKGS.
Sponges	8	10
First Aid		
MERTHIOLATE	1 BOTTLE	0
BANDAIDS	∝	∝
ADHESIVE TAPE	1 ROLL	2 ROLLS
Miscellaneous		
STEIN BODY MAKEUP — GOLD	0	1 QT.
" " " SILVER	½ QT.	0
GOLD SEQUINS	0	1 PKG.
THREAD — WHITE	0	2 SPOOLS
Wigs, Falls, and Toupees		
AUBURN FALLS	2	0
BALD WIG	1	0
18th CENTURY WIGS		RENT 6

Figure 19.

Date: _____

<u>MAKEUP OUTLINE</u>

ACTOR: _John Doe_

CHARACTER: _Richard III_

PLAY: _Richard III_

NAME, COLOR, DESCRIPTION, BRAND	ON HAND
Foundation: Factor #7-A Grease	OK
Stein Neutral Powder	OK
Powder Puff, Brush	OK
Shadowing and Highlighting:	No-
Factor #9 Grease	
Stein Clown-White	OK
Factor #6N Panstik	No-
Eye Makeup: Black & Brown Pencils ⅛ Stein	OK
Rouge and Lipstick: Mehron #11 Moist Rouge	OK
Hair: Black Shoulder=Length Wig	To Be Rented
Black Crêpe Hair	OK
Spirit Gum & Remover	OK

Figure 19 (Continued)

Prosthesis:	
Nose putty — Stein	OK
Derma - wax	OK
Thread	OK

Special:	
Stein stage blood	No
Black tooth wax	No.

Wig measurements:

Around head — 21½

Front hairline to nape — 14

Top of head (ear-to-ear) — 11½

Forehead (ear-to-ear) - 12

Wig to be dressed in straight "page-boy" fashion.

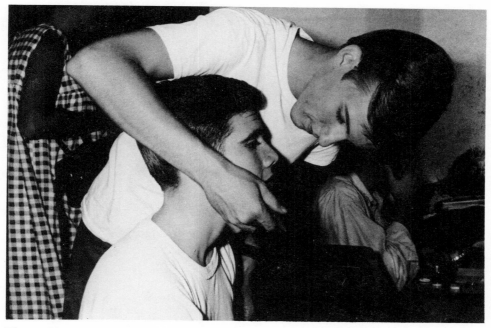

Figure 20 *A young makeup artist at Southwest Miami High School, Florida, prepares an actor-colleague for his appearance.*

supply, although everyone who uses it should assist in those jobs.

A "collection" of makeup is temporary, in that its contents increase with necessary purchases and decrease with use. It is a good idea to make regular inventories of makeup supplies, whether personal or institutional. Figure 18 is a sample inventory sheet for a large collection of makeup, and can be adapted for use by a group or an individual to fit specific purposes. Figure 19 is a check list of materials needed for a particular part and is meant to aid the individual actor preparing a role.

It is well to remember that time must be allowed for makeup supplies on order to arrive, even on a "rush" order. Also, you must take into consideration the fact that the firm from which you order your supplies may need to order them from a wholesaler. Therefore, in ordering and maintaining makeup supplies, it might be a wise procedure to allow just twice as much time as you would suppose might ordinarily be required between your order and ultimate receipt of the goods.

Once your makeup kit is assembled, you are ready for the fun . . . and hard work . . . of application!

Chapter IV

THE ACTOR MEETS THE CHARACTER: FACE TO FACE

"What beard were I best to play it in?"
Shakespeare, *A Midsummer Night's Dream,* Act I, Scene ii.

Congratulations! You have, at last, passed through the preliminary agonies of script study, the preparation of an audition, the audition itself, and you have been cast in a part. Your friends probably envy you all the fun you are going to have, and, indeed, your work on the play should be filled with fun for you. But you are also embarking on a period of hard, intensive work, if you are at all sincere about wanting to please an audience with a fine performance.

A most important part of the hard work that goes into the preparation of a play is the design and rehearsal of the makeup. When an audience sees a theatrical performance, as in the case of an iceberg, only about one-ninth of the total mass is actually seen. Many people work many long, hard hours to create the brief performance seen by the audience.

Every element of a theatrical produc-tion must be carefully *designed.* Included, as each actor's preparation of his part, is his makeup. Well in advance of performance dates, even, in some cases, well in advance of casting, the director must design the actors' movements and vocal patterns, the scenic designer must prepare his working drawings and plans, drawings and patterns must be made for costumes, and so on. Unfortunately, makeup design is frequently left until the time of dress rehearsals, or virtually too late for practicing and altering it. For self-evident reasons, that is foolish.

One of the most important intangibles with which an actor must deal is self-confidence. Stage fright is an occupational hazard to which all actors are subject, absolutely regardless of whether they are going onstage for the first time ever in a junior-high-school production, or playing the lead for the thousandth time in a Broadway hit. Many actors of long-standing fame have surprised interviewers and readers of magazines or newspapers by asserting that they worry when they do *not* have stage fright. It frequently serves as the stimulus needed to keep the actor "on his toes" at every moment during a performance. That can be extremely critical, as anyone will tell you who has ever participated in an exhausting season of stock or repertory, or in a play whose run is of long duration.

In order to maintain a good balance between the kind of stage fright that stimulates the energy and excitement necessary to a strong, lively performance, and the debilitating kind that paralyzes the actor and ruins his performance, care must be taken to have everything connected with the performance as nearly perfect as is possible in the theatre. Because theatrical production is made up of the efforts of many human beings, and because all human beings are subject to error, things can and do go wrong. In every theatre person's bag of anecdotes are many stories of forgotten lines, falling scenery, tearing costumes, electrical failures, and so forth. They are very funny in retrospect, but can cause a great deal of anguish at the time they actually occur.

"Trouble-shooting" possible problems in advance is one of the things that gives stage managers ulcers. Every actor should make an effort to foresee and prevent problems. What problems, you might ask, could occur with makeup? Do you want to be the actor who leaves his mustache on the leading lady's lip following a romantic embrace? Or would

you care to be the character actress who, in the middle of a deeply serious scene, puts her hand to her head, and sends up clouds of hair-whitening powder gleaming in the beam of the stage lights? Unthinkable is the prosthetic nose dropping off in the middle of a soliloquy (but possible)!

The rehearsal period is the time to make mistakes, study them, and, hopefully, correct them. As the rehearsal period progresses toward the performance dates, the tempo, the tension, the activity, and the fatigue become increasingly intense. Therefore, the earlier you can practice and experiment with your makeup, the more time and energy you will have to devote to other problems as opening night draws near.

At the first reading rehearsal or rehearsals, the director will probably give you a sense of style he wishes to create with the production, the overall balance he hopes to achieve among the characterizations, and possibly will show you early working drawings for the scenery and costumes. In experiencing the interplay of the earliest rehearsals, you should quickly gain a good feeling for the character you are to portray. It is then that you should begin your first experiments in the makeup for your character.

If the director, or perhaps the wardrobe director or makeup crew chief, does not volunteer information and equipment to you in connection with your makeup, it might not be amiss to request their ideas on it, and permission to begin the design of your makeup.

In many school, college, and amateur groups will be found either a makeup crew or a makeup chairman. In most cases, having one person in charge of makeup is a splendid idea, because that person can coordinate the styles of many into one overall style, help less-experienced actors with the various techniques of makeup, and inventory and order supplies. Except in cases of an entire cast requiring elaborate or unusual makeup (as in Figures 2, 13, 21, and 22), or many difficult changes throughout the play, as might be found in *The Fourposter, Victoria Regina,* or *The Apple Tree,* generally one person should suffice.

Each actor should be able to apply his own makeup, with careful guidance and practice throughout the rehearsal period under the direction of the makeup chairman. A dressing room is a tense, crowded, hectic place during dress rehearsals, and the fewer people in it, the better. All too often people apply to a director to be members of a makeup crew simply in order to be around the excitement of dress rehearsals and performances and attend cast parties, without having to spend the long, demanding, and sometimes tedious hours required in other areas of theatrical production.

Having established the need to be well prepared to apply your makeup, you should review the materials and ideas of Chapters I and II, then prepare your design. Even a simple "straight" juvenile or ingenue makeup will need thoughtful preparation and practice.

Time is of the essence in the theatre. There is just never enough. As you begin your makeup applications, time yourself carefully. If your makeup is at all difficult, and especially if you are unfamiliar with some techniques, do not be misled by the typical "half-hour call," which requires you to be present in the theatre one-half hour before curtain time. Most actors allow themselves one-half hour *more* than the time required to get into costume and makeup to compensate for emergencies and nerves.

As you design your makeup, you should consult with the director and/or the makeup chairman, and quite possibly the costume and lighting designers as well. If you begin early enough in the rehearsal period, those people will have time and mental energy to devote to you; later on, they may be too harassed with the problems of coordinating the entire production to give you more than cursory attention.

You should be fully aware of the size of the theatre, even its shape. The makeup you will use for a 1,500-seat auditorium will never do in an arena-style production before an audience of 150.

At the present time, and for some years past, it is usual to hear that lighting must be planned to convey atmosphere. Although this aspect of lighting must be considered, it seems to me that on the whole atmosphere is best conveyed by the actor, and his makeup, because in theatre the actor is the vital instrument, not the stage designer, nor the electrician.[7]

That statement is true, but the actor dares not discount lighting as an adjunct

---

[7] Yoti Lane, *Stage Make-Up* (Minneapolis, Minnesota: The Northwestern Press, 1950), p. 13.

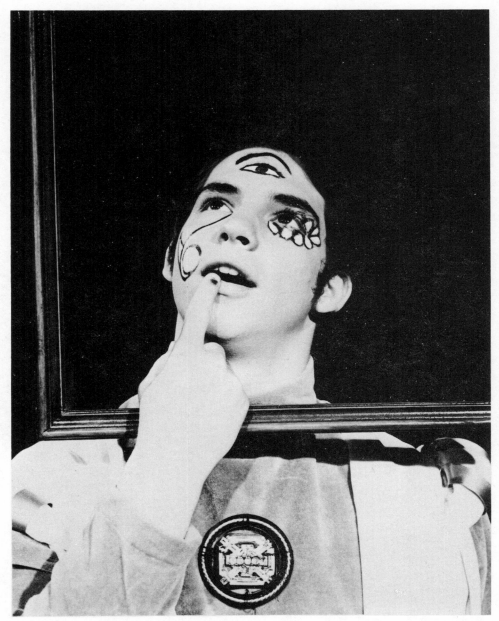

Figure 21 *An example of imaginative fantasy makeup for a production of* The Chairs *at Memphis State University.*

Figure 22 *At Chicago's Alvernia High School, a few simple strokes of makeup combined with adroit costuming turn people into rabbits in* The House at Pooh Corner.

to his performance. If the playscript demands an exterior night scene (and it is staggering to think how many do), both actor and lighting designer have a real technical problem on their hands. The actual color of moonlight has never been scientifically determined, as have other direct and reflected colors. The various colors of media used in lighting such a scene can wreak havoc with a makeup that looks fine in daylight or interior lighting. If the overall "wash" of light on a stage contains a great deal of pink, the prettiest shade of green eyeshadow will become a dull brown.

Although most problems arising from the effect of lights on makeup are not readily apparent until the first technical dress rehearsal, if both lighting designer and actors are aware of potential problems at the outset of rehearsals, they can experiment with color combinations at leisure and thus prevent a lot of panic.

The costume designer is an invaluable ally in matters of period style or "exotic" designs. To keep the costumer an ally, and not create an enemy, you will need to treat his costumes as well as, if not better than, you would manage your personal wardrobe. In productions requiring fantasy or other extreme characters, the costume designer may well design the makeup as an inherent part of the costume, as in the animal costumes in Figures 13 and 22. In his research for period plays, he will have automatically come across makeup requirements as well, such as the wearing of beauty spots. An excellent source for your own

research in period makeup and wigs is Corson's *Stage Makeup*.[8]

A note of caution is in order here: Be *very* sure of your advisers when creating your makeup. Ideally, you should take the advice only of authorized personnel involved with the production, as discussed above. If you discuss your makeup with friends, make sure they are friends whose background and experience in the theatre are extensive and reliable.

No young beginning actor is helped by the friend or relative whose well-meaning but misguided reaction to his makeup is, "You're *not* going to wear all those lines and smudges on your face in front of all those people, are you?" And pity the poor young actress whose adoring but theatrically uncritical mother says, "Take off those eyelashes, and all that rouge. You look *cheap*."

An important factor that must be taken up with the director right after casting is hair style. That is especially true of men. With the easy availability of crêpe hair and wigs, a man need not grow his own hair if he does not wish to do so. However, some feel more comfortable with a mustache or sideburns of their own; even, if there is time to grow one, a beard. By the same token, a man should not get a "bulldog" or "GI" haircut if a slightly longer style would be more appropriate.

In the event any haircut is needed, it should be done well in advance of performances, as the shaved area on the back of the neck shows up distractingly

---

[8] Op. cit., pp. 303–14; 377–427.

bright under stage lights, and cannot be adequately obliterated by makeup.

If at all possible, shaving should be avoided for several hours before applying makeup; ideally the morning shave should be the last one. Under no circumstances should a man shave immediately before making up. Makeup, and especially beard adhesive on a tender, freshly shaved face, can cause an extremely painful irritation, particularly to nicks, scrapes, or cuts.

The theatre, throughout history, has had an unfortunate reputation for frivolity, if not outright rowdiness on the part of its personnel, especially actors. People outside of the theatre seldom realize that actors are dedicated, hard-working artist-craftsmen who, in order to give their finest performances, must combine the stamina of a well-trained athlete with the scholarship of a professor. The more professional the actor (and is not every actor's goal the achievement of the highest possible level of professionalism?), the more considerate he is of others. An actor does not work alone. He depends upon other people, who in turn depend upon him for maximum effectiveness in performance.

As is the case in any walk of life in which people interact with one another, the theatre has certain rules of etiquette. Despite what many people think, a theatrical presentation is an exercise in hard discipline. Precision before an audience requires the obedience, on the part of all involved, to a strong, rational ethic.

The very heart of theatrical etiquette is found in the dressing rooms. If you have ever shared a room with a brother, sister, or roommate you will understand the kind of tension involved in such an arrangement, particularly if one is fastidious and the other sloppy. In a dressing room, you will share with from one to a dozen comparative strangers a "home away from home." There is simply never enough space in the theatre, no matter how well planned or essentially spacious yours is. You will find cramped quarters everywhere, but above all in the dressing room. Nervous tension and the constant necessity to hurry combine to make a difficult situation almost intolerable.

For the above reasons, courtesy must begin at home, in your "home away from home." The floor, the dressing table, and chairs are not places to store costumes. In order for you to look your best, your costume should look its best, and it will do so if it is carefully hung up, and all accessories neatly stored in their proper place every minute they are not being worn.

How would you like to appear onstage wearing a costume badly wrinkled, with smudges of makeup on it, and a squashed hat? The old saw, "A place for everything, and everything in its place," could not have a more realistic application than in a theatrical dressing room.

You will in all likelihood find that you will have to line up and take turns: at the dressing table, at the mirror, at the washbasin. If you have arrived at the theatre early enough to compensate for waiting as you prepare to go onstage, there should be no problem. But if a maddening sense of frustrating urgency surrounds your makeup and dressing procedures (as it almost always will), you must learn to utilize the greatest possible willpower to avoid being rude. Hostile aggressiveness neither solves problems nor gets the work done sooner; on the contrary, it delays smooth preparation and compounds the existing nervous tension.

Your makeup table should be neat, clean, and orderly, with each piece of equipment where you can readily find it. Before leaving the theatre following a rehearsal or performance, it is a good idea to arrange your equipment and your costume carefully, so that all will be ready when you must use them again next day. At that time, you will discover things that need repairs or replacement, and can inform the proper personnel. If you have run out of some makeup item, what good will it do to run about hysterically fifteen minutes before curtain time trying to replace it? But if you have told the right person a day ahead of time, the chances are it can be replaced or a substitute provided. In *Hamlet,* Polonius tells his son, "Neither a borrower nor a lender be." That is excellent advice, but at times you *must* be a borrower of makeup, and if the item is returned promptly and in good shape, the chances are you will not have to suffer when the time comes for you to be a lender.

Excitement always abounds in a dressing room, and inevitably a good deal of chatter. But to enjoy your work, and to share your enjoyment and excitement with others in the company, need not include boisterous yelling, singing, whistling, and stupid pranks. It is just plain foolish to waste your priceless energy, every ounce of which you will need in performance, before an unwilling dressing-room audience.

Spills and smears do occur, and should be cleaned up immediately, or at least as soon as possible. It would be the most basic kind of courtesy to warn others in your dressing room if you have gotten makeup on the floor, particularly if broken glass is involved.

Nobody likes to use a dirty, smeared washbasin or shower. Enough said?

One aspect of the dress rehearsal period, which most actors regard as an "evil necessity," is the photograph call. Some photographers are capable, through experimentation and experience, of photographing an entire production during a closed dress rehearsal, using available filtered theatre lights. Such photographs, naturally, are the best, the most representative of the actual performance. But such photographers are, unfortunately, few and far between. For most theatrical purposes, photographs must be made with unfiltered lights or flashbulbs. Often, the photographs must be slowly, agonizingly posed following one of the last dress rehearsals.

When the photograph call is posted, you should check as to what kind of photography will be used. If white, unfiltered lighting, or stage lighting "boosted" with additional white floodlights, will be used, your makeup can remain essentially the same. If flashbulbs are used, you will have to tone it down, in terms of lines and contrasts.

The director, or the photographer himself, should be able to advise you on the amount, severity, the "theatricality" of the makeup you should use for photographs. Figure 23 shows an actress in full makeup, whose efforts under the glare of the photographer's lights are all too evident. It is one thing to photograph a makeup for purposes of analyzing it; quite another to prepare publicity shots in which the makeup is theatrically conspicuous.

Having become acquainted with certain aspects of makeup art that should readily become second nature to you, you are now ready to learn its craft. It is a difficult craft to describe, not unlike Professor Parkinson's famous test of describing a corkscrew without using the hands; but once you have practiced with the materials themselves, many aspects of makeup, which seem like formidable problems on paper, will seem easy to you.

Application of the Foundation

Having selected, or having had selected for you, the color and type of foundation makeup, this item will be the first you will apply, and should, therefore, be readily available to you on the dressing table.

Before applying the foundation, you must be certain that all street makeup, soil, medication, and after-shave materials have been carefully and thoroughly removed from your face. Particularly if you have long hair, you should bind your hair back and away from your face with a scarf or towel. You may also want to wear a makeup cape, smock, or towel around your shoulders.

If your foundation, or base makeup, is to be the stick-type greasepaint, you must first apply an extremely thin coat of cold cream or mineral oil to the entire area that is to take the makeup. Most people find it easier to apply the coating fairly liberally, then wipe off the excess. If too much is used, your face will gleam like a beacon, even through the powder, and perspiration, natural under the heat of the lights, will become an uncomfortable and unwieldy problem.

Peeling back the paper in which the grease sticks are usually wrapped, stroke the makeup on with a fairly light touch. You should use perhaps two strokes on each cheek, one on the forehead, one on the nose, and one on the chin, with equivalent amounts going on the neck, ears, arms, and hands. With clean hands, gently smooth and blend the makeup away from the strokes to cover the entire area. At first you may have to remove some of the makeup, if it seems to be caked on in spots, or you may have to add strokes from the makeup stick in places where you have used it too sparingly. It is one of those things you learn with time, practice, and experience.

If you are using the tube-type greasepaint, which already contains the oily lubricant, you will *not* need to apply cream or oil to your face before the application of the makeup. Instead, simply squeeze about an inch of makeup into the palm of one hand, then with the other (both hands being clean), daub the makeup onto your face in equidistant dots (see Figure 24, 25).

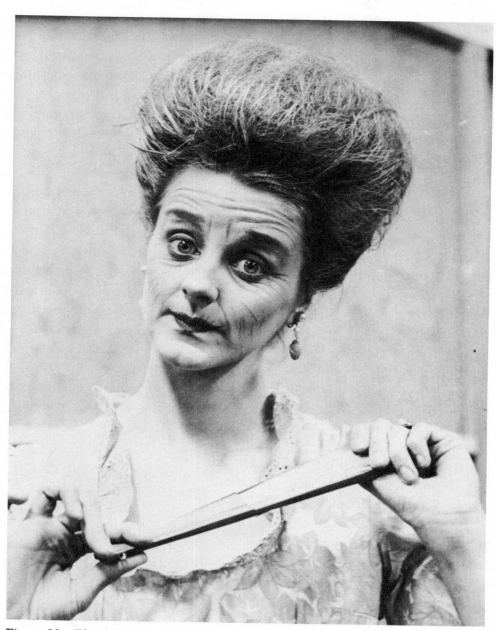

Figure 23 *The details of Mrs. Malaprop's makeup in* The Rivals *at Memphis State University are perhaps too much in evidence, owing to the intensity of the lighting.*

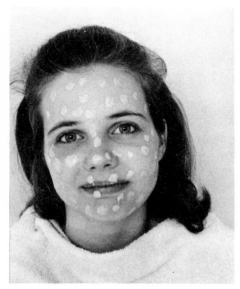

Figure 24 *The first step in applying greasepaint: Diana Novak of Missouri Western College applies dots of grease all over her face.*

Once the dots have been applied, spread and blend them over the whole surface, just as you might have done with the strokes from the stick greasepaint. The makeup, again, should be neither too heavy nor too light, and you may have to remove some of it, or make careful additions.

The necessity for making a habit of cleaning your hands will become self-evident as you practice makeup. You should always have a towel or tissue handy for cleaning your hands before each application. In some cases, you will actually need to wash your hands with soap and water between procedures. The first time you attempt to make a highlight with a very light color, just after having blended a dark brown or black shadow with the same fingers, you will understand what the hand cleaning is all about.

To use the semigrease, semicake foun-dation, such as Factor's "Pan-Stik," the same method should be used as for the grease stick, but *without* the prior application of cream or oil.

In using pancake makeup, which is probably the most comfortable kind to wear, a clean sponge and clear water are required. The ideal sponge for such makeup is a natural sponge, approximately 2″ in diameter. Such sponges are quite expensive, however, and not always easy to come by, so it may be necessary to use a rubber sponge, or one made from some other synthetic material.

The sponge should be soaked in water, then wrung in the fingertips until it is just barely damp. Too much or too little water in the sponge will tend to streak the makeup. Here is still another technique that can be learned only through experience.

The dampened sponge should be stroked across the cake of makeup, and

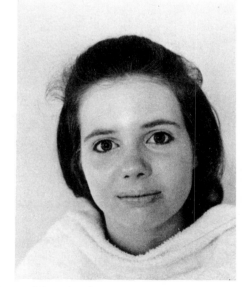

Figure 25 *The dots of greasepaint are blended to create a masklike covering of color.*

the makeup quickly applied in even, steady strokes, blending each new stroke carefully with the last. It is applied thus until the entire area has been covered.

If the makeup is streaked, it can generally be smoothed and blended by going over it with a clean, slightly dampened sponge.

The cautionary remarks about clean hands are applicable to the sponges in the use of cake makeup. You will probably need two or three sponges but, particularly if you are limited to only one, make sure it is carefully rinsed out between applications.

Liquid makeup is best applied with a clean sponge. If large areas of the body are to be covered with liquid makeup, such as the back or the legs, then a larger size sponge can be used. It is generally best to pour the makeup out of the bottle and into a basin, so that the sponge can be more easily dipped in and wrung out while applying the makeup. Then what is left over can be poured back into the bottle through a funnel.

Commercial preparations for street wear generally come with their own applicators and instructions on how to apply them. As was pointed out in Chapter III, their usefulness is limited in the theatre.

Once the foundation has been applied, you may be a little startled at your appearance. You will seem to be wearing a mask: Your face will be quite expressionless. In fact, you may even think you look a little ill. In applying the foundation color thoroughly and completely to all exposed areas (no scrimping on ears, back of neck, hands and arms), you will

have done what a painter must do in preparing a canvas: created a uniform, matte surface upon which you will have perfect control over the painted details you wish to add.

If you intend to wear a beard, mustache, sideburns, or a wig, you should not apply foundation makeup to the areas that will require the use of adhesive. Some actors find, particularly at the outset, that making a light line with eyebrow pencil around those areas helps them to remember to leave them clean of makeup.

Before moving on to the next step, double-check your foundation to see that it is smooth, uniform, and covers all of your skin that will show. Remember, *you* may not see the back of your neck and ears, but the audience will, and nothing is more irritating than to look at an actor who has left a "line of demarcation" between his makeup and his own skin.

SHADING AND HIGHLIGHTING

Having "blanked out" your face with foundation makeup, you will now begin to restore its dimensionality with, in some cases, some improvements over Mother Nature. That is accomplished with shading and highlighting.

Many people forget that shadows and highlights are like two sides of a coin: you cannot have one without the other. If you look at any three-dimensional form under a single, directed source of light, you will see that that is true. Where the light strikes the surface, there is a highlight. The surface also casts a shadow of itself.

Theatrical lighting tends to "wash out" natural highlights and shadows. With its intense wattage coming from in front, behind, overhead, both sides, and even sometimes below, contours that would, in daylight or average room lighting, tend to create highlights and shadows are canceled out by the multi-directional light.

With that in mind, scenery painters take great pains to paint contours onto flat and even shaped surfaces. Costumers sometimes find it necessary to paint shadings onto costumes, if the lighting seems to make them flat and unnatural. And you, as makeup artist, must restore the natural contours of your face, which the lighting and the flattening effect of foundation makeup have all but obliterated.

At this point, it might be a good idea to review the material of Chapter I on the anatomical details of the face. Using your senses of sight and touch together, you should be able to create a natural dimensionality on your "painted" face.

The highlighting color should be one or two shades lighter than the foundation, and the shading color one or two shades darker. If you use shades much lighter or darker than the foundation, the extreme contrast will look phony.

For shading and highlighting colors, you *must* use the same kind of makeup as was used for the foundation: If you used grease for the foundation, use grease for the shading; if you used pancake for the foundation, use pancake for the shading. Trying to mix the two types beyond minimum limitations will reveal inconsistencies in texture and create problems for powdering.

For some odd reason, most actors prefer to apply shadows first, followed by highlights. Perhaps it has something to do with the fact that one can see shadows (lines and indentations) more readily than highlights, and can use the former as guidelines for applying the latter.

Having studied the contours of your own face as prescribed in Chapter I, you know that the major shadows on your face fall at the temples, the sides of the nose, and in the hollows of the cheeks. Smaller ones occur under the nose and beneath the lower lip. The shadows and highlights surrounding the eyes will be taken up later.

The shading and highlighting makeup is applied in the same way as the foundation, but once it is applied, you must carefully "feather," or blend, the edges of the new color, so that a harsh, obvious line will not indicate the edges of the shading. With greasepaint, using clean fingertips, you should blend away from the spot where the makeup was originally applied most heavily (the darkest part of a shadow; the brightest part of a highlight) in radiating strokes, constantly smoothing and blending until it is impossible to see where the shading begins and the foundation leaves off. With pancake makeup, a damp sponge is used for the blending. The shading technique is a bit more difficult to learn with pancake than it is with greasepaint, but practice, as always, will make perfect.

The principal highlights are to be found on the forehead, across the tops of the cheekbones, down the bridge of the nose, and on the chin (see Figure 26).

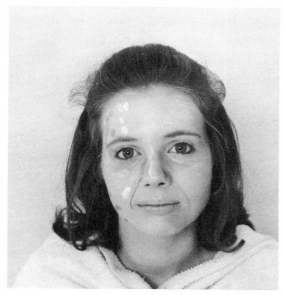

Figure 26 *On one side of the actress' face, dots of shading and highlight color, and a line from the side of the nose to the mouth have been applied. On the other side of her face, the colors have been blended by "feathering" the harsh edges and smoothing them into the base color.*

A rational and clever use of highlights and shadows can do much to correct real or imagined deficiencies of an actor's face. If an effect of minor widening or narrowing of certain features is desired, it can be done with shading paint, thus eliminating the necessity for difficult, complex prosthetic makeup. You simply need to "cheat" a little in applying your makeup: widening or lengthening a highlight tends to widen or lengthen the feature; widening or lengthening the shadow tends to make the feature appear narrower or shorter. This is something with which you can experiment at your leisure. To inspect the results as an audience might see them, squint your

eyes just enough to put them slightly out of focus as you look in the mirror. If you are nearsighted, simply remove your glasses.

Rouge and Lipstick

If the character you are portraying is either very ill, or an indoors-type older person, the chances are you will have little, if anything, to do with rouge. Otherwise, a blush of rouge on the cheeks will indicate a healthy, natural coloring. Men as well as women should keep that in mind.

Rouge comes in two forms: moist and dry. The moist rouge has a consistency slightly thicker than tube greasepaint, and should be applied in much the same way as greasepaint: a single dot on each cheek, which is then smoothed out and blended with a clean fingertip.

Dry rouge generally comes with an applicator like a miniature powder puff, which should be discarded. The best and most subtle way to apply dry rouge is with a soft-bristled, round, watercolor brush of about ¼″ to ½″ diameter. The brush is stroked on the rouge cake, then vigorously shaken to get rid of excess rouge, then stroked lightly onto the cheeks. Using the little puff applicator tends to leave an unnatural, hard-edged appearance, which, in some cases, might be desirable, such as in portraying an eccentric old woman who uses too much makeup.

You must be very careful with the placement of rouge: applied near the nose, it makes the face appear narrower;

applied nearer to the ears, it widens the face.

Lipstick can be either the type readily available in any drugstore or notions shop, or it can be applied from a jar of moist rouge. No matter which is used, it should be carefully applied with a brush, in order to obtain exactly the lip outline desired. Once again, "cheating" can create various effects: One or both lips can be either narrowed or thickened by an adroit use of the lipstick brush. The ideal brush for this purpose is the Oriental natural-bristle-and-bamboo lettering brush, which has a sturdy and refined point on the bristles.

After the lipstick has been applied, it should be gently blotted on a tissue to remove the excess. If kissing is involved in the play, in order for the lady not to leave a smudge of red on the gentleman's face, she should blot and powder the lipstick repeatedly until it is "set."

For the most part, men do not need to wear lipstick on the stage, unless the theatre is extremely large, or the lighting particularly intense.

Contrary to popular belief (and certain old-fashioned books on makeup), a line, drawn in dark-brown or black pencil, should *not* be used to outline the lips. Supposedly it defines the lips, but in actuality it serves no other purpose than to make the actor look as if he had been eating licorice before going onstage.

If a man is playing a part requiring him to wear grotesque or stylized lipstick, such as an eighteenth-century fop, he should experiment with the use of it a few times before dress rehearsal, and

become accustomed to the blotting and powdering procedure.

Extremely pale lipsticks in the pink or peach hues will generally be lost on the stage. Regardless of what color lipstick a woman might wear on the street, her stage lipstick should be a fairly bright, true red.

EYE MAKEUP

Enhancing the natural expressiveness of the eyes, or altering their appearance entirely, involves some of the trickiest, most delicate techniques in makeup. Much attention and practice should be given to this aspect of makeup, for the eyes are the most powerful instrument the actor possesses.

If false eyelashes are to be used, they should be applied first. The actress wearing them should have had prior experience with them, in order to become accustomed to their weight on her eyelids and to the peculiar stiff, scratchy feeling they impart. The first time they are worn, they should be carefully trimmed by another person with scissors, so that they follow the contours of the natural eyelashes. Afterward, they must be kept in a box with "right" and "left" clearly marked.

Although some false eyelashes are packaged with adhesive included, not all of them are. Even if glue comes with them, there is generally not enough to last for several wearings, and the most reliable adhesive to use is surgical adhesive. It can be obtained in any drugstore, can be used also for prosthetic and crêpe hair attachments, and will not harm the eyes.

The adhesive should be applied with a toothpick or matchstick evenly and sparingly to the base of the false eyelashes. Then the false eyelashes should be placed just above the roots of the natural lashes on the upper lid, and held in place until the adhesive has dried.

Adhesive should not be permitted to accumulate on the base of the false eyelashes, as it collects makeup and dirt and weakens the holding power of further layers of adhesive. It can generally be rubbed or pulled off, like rubber cement. Failing this, it can be removed with acetone (or fingernail polish remover, which is basically acetone).

Men do not usually wear false eyelashes, but may find it necessary to wear mascara, particularly if they have blond or red hair and light eyelashes that will not register in the theatre.

Mascara comes in liquid and dry cake forms, the most commonly used in the theatre being the latter. The applicator for mascara is generally a small, stiff-bristled brush that looks something like a miniature toothbrush. Some of the liquid types have a spiral wand applicator.

If dry cake mascara is used, the brush should be thoroughly moistened, then stroked across the mascara cake. The mascara will form a thick liquid, the consistency of paste, and should be applied as such. Too much water will make it run; not enough will render it impossible to apply.

The mascara should be stroked onto the underside of the upper lashes, start-ing at the roots of the lashes and stroking upward and outward toward the tips. It must be done with a steady hand and with great care, as it is quite painful to get mascara in your eyes. If that should happen, however, the eyes can be quickly washed out with clear water.

"Lining" the eyes is, as the word implies, a method of emphasizing and dramatizing the eyes with a dark line. The eyes are somewhat shadowed by the ridge of the eyebrow, particularly if a lot of overhead lighting is used, and must be outlined in order to register to an audience.

To line the eyes, the skin of the eyelid must be stretched taut with a fingertip at the outer corner of the eye. Then, using either an eyebrow pencil or a pointed brush dipped in liner color, the line is made across the eyelid as closely as possible to the roots of the eyelashes from the point nearest the nose to the outside edge of the eye (see Figure 27).

If the lower as well as the upper lid is lined (which it need not always be), the line should begin at about the middle of the eye and extend to the outer corner.

A word of caution to wearers of contact lenses: The eyes must be lined before inserting the lenses, because the stretching of the eyelid will cause a lens to pop out.

If eyeshadow is used, it should be applied before the eyeliner. Men should not, as a rule, use eyeshadow, but both men and women may wish to highlight the orbit of the eye, particularly if the eyes are deep-set. Blue, brown, or lavender eyeshadow should be applied

Figure 27 *Miss Novak stretches the eyelid with one hand while applying eye lining with the other.* (**Photographs by Lynne Anderson**)

with a brush from the roots of the eyelashes to approximately the middle of the eye orbit. Above the eyeshadow, a highlight color or a light shade of rouge should be applied up to the base of the eyebrow.

If the natural line of the eyebrows is used, it inevitably needs to be darkened, except in an old-age makeup, when the brows are made to look gray. Either an eyebrow pencil, or a brush dipped in dark-brown or black grease liner, is used to darken the eyebrows. If it becomes necessary to change the natural line of the eyebrow, the hairs of the eyebrow should be heavily coated with a layer of soap (an ordinary cake of toilet soap slightly moistened) or a fairly thick application of spirit gum. The coating is then covered with foundation color, and the false eyebrows drawn over it.

An "old wives' tale" persists in the theatre regarding the use of red dots at the inner corners of the eyes. In the days when gas lighting was used, with its greenish glow, it was necessary to daub small spots of rouge at the inner corners of the eyes to make them appear natural. In this day and age of filtered incandescent lighting, such a procedure is entirely unnecessary, and serves either to make the eyes appear crossed, at worst, or to make the wearer look as if he is simply wearing red dots in the corners of his eyes.

AGE MAKEUP

"Growing old gracefully" is one of the privileges of the makeup artist, all the more attractive since the aging process can be erased with soap and water following a performance.

Gravity, both of the Newtonian kind and that conferred upon age by experience, tends to make all of the facial muscles sag downward. Muscles lose their tone, and the flesh over them wrinkles.

To create an illusion of age on a firm young face is a difficult, complex process. Wrinkles are not just lines on a firm surface; they are indentations in the skin, upon which light creates highlights and shadows.

The loss of tone in the muscles causes the natural shadows to deepen, and thus the highlights become more pronounced. Following the application of the base makeup, the highlighting and shadowing must be done with great care, exaggerating the muscular sagging observed in a study of either old people themselves, or photographs of them. The shadows at the temples will tend to deepen, a puffiness will develop under the eyes, and, perhaps most noticeable, a sagging and thickening at the jowls and across the front of the throat will form (see Figure 5).

Without using prosthetic makeup, the sagging quality of old age can be only suggested. If prosthetic devices are not used, cooperation from the costume department may be sought in masking the telltale throat with a high-necked costume. Men can, of course, hide the problem of the aged jawline and throat behind a beard.

Blending is of extreme importance in applying both broad areas of shading and the finer lines that represent wrinkles. The hard edges of lines must be "feathered" carefully to avoid the sketched-on, self-conscious appearance of being made up (see Figure 23). Also, to accommodate the natural mobility of the face during the speaking of lines and the changing of facial expression, the wrinkles must follow the natural lines formed by the face itself. In other words, before you draw lines on the forehead, you should raise your eyebrows as high as they will go, and follow the lines thus formed. For the creation of "crow's-feet" and other lines around the eyes, it is necessary to squint hard, as if looking into a strong light. For the deepening lines around the mouth, a wide grin is in order, and to indicate the fine lines formed by loss of teeth, or the part-time wearing of dentures, the lips must be pursed to form a "u." A special word of warning about the latter: They must be extremely subtle, and very well blended,

or they will tend to appear phony. They must also be heavily powdered to avoid smearing; in short, if possible, it is better to do without them.

Some people have extremely taut flesh on the skull and over the bones of the facial mask, and their faces do not form natural lines, no matter how much they may grimace, scowl, and grin. In such cases, it is sometimes necessary to squeeze or gather the flesh with the fingers in order to ascertain where and how natural lines might fall.

A good device that will contribute to an illusion of age is the graying or whitening of the hair and eyebrows. Hair-coloring materials were discussed in Chapter III. In using aerosol-spray materials for streaking or covering all of the hair, care must be taken not to spray near an open flame, and the eyes must be protected from the spray by shielding them with either the hand or a piece of stiff paper.

To age the eyebrows, clown white or white greasepaint should be stroked on *against* the natural growth of the hair; that is, from the outside edges inward, toward the nose.

PROSTHETIC MAKEUP

The ideal makeup for transforming a young face into an old one is latex prosthesis. Stock prosthetic pieces can be purchased from major multipurpose theatrical supply houses that sell or rent costumes, wigs, scenery, lighting equipment, and so forth. They are not altogether satisfactory, as they cannot fit the individual face as well as pieces actually tailor-made for it. For the novice, however, they are easier than the rather arduous process required for making prosthetic attachments.

Figure 5 illustrates an excellent prosthetic makeup for old age created by Dick Smith, S.M.A. Richard Corson's *Stage Makeup* contains two particularly detailed chapters on prosthetic makeup that are invaluable as guides to a difficult art.[9]

The starting point for latex prosthesis is the making of a "life mask," or plaster casting of the actor's face. The making of a life mask is described in detail in Chapter V. The actor who owns a life mask of his face can save himself considerable time and effort in the long run, despite the discomfort and messiness of the original casting. Prosthetic pieces and latex bases for beards and mustaches can be made on the mask, as well as leisure-time experiments with various forms of makeup.

Once the life mask has been made, the latex prosthetic pieces can be modeled directly on it, or, in some cases, on a negative mold made from the positive life mask with clay or plaster. Nose- and chinpieces can be hollow, built up on a clay extension casting made on the life mask contours. They are ideal for such characters as Cyrano de Bergerac and Pinocchio, as they are light in weight, comfortable to wear, and permit the actor great mobility in facial expression and head movement. Enough layers of latex must be painted over the clay model to assure strength and stability of the piece. Too many layers may alter

the shape desired, or make the piece too heavy. "Just the right amount" is, alas, another of those maddening aspects of the art of makeup based partly on experience and partly on instinct.

High, pointed elf ears such as those that might be worn by Puck in *A Midsummer Night's Dream* may be made in the same way on a casting of the actor's ear.

Flabby cheeks, jowls, and throat must have a somewhat more substantial base in order to be effective. Instead of hollow latex shells, the latex forms must be filled with foamed or whipped latex. It creates a little additional weight, but allows the actor freedom of facial movement, without the fear of denting or crushing the prosthetic piece.

Before attempting to make latex prosthetic pieces, perhaps the best procedure for the beginning makeup artist to follow would be to rent or purchase simple stock pieces and carefully examine their construction, keeping in mind the plaster cast or clay model used as a basis.

Latex pieces are attached to the face prior to the application of any other makeup. On a clean, dry skin surface, and on the surface of the piece that will adhere to the face, surgical adhesive should be applied liberally. After allowing it to dry for a few seconds, or until it has become "tacky," the piece is pressed into place and held firmly until the adhesive has had plenty of time to dry completely. The piece should then be gently pulled, to test the effectiveness of the adhesion. Excess adhesive that has spread beyond the edges of the piece can be rolled off the skin with the fin-

[9] Op. cit., pp. 160–204.

gers, the same way as rubber cement can be rolled from paper.

The most commonly used makeup item for creating false noses and chins is nose putty. Warning: It is also uncomfortable, messy to use, and unreliable. If a production is to be performed only once or twice, and expense is a major consideration (when is it not?), nose putty will probably serve quite adequately.

It must be applied before other makeup on a clean, dry skin. It must be softened to a workable consistency by a combination of heat and kneading. Generally, the heat of the palms of the hands is sufficient to make it workable, although if it has been exposed to cold, the softening process can be accelerated by heating it with a hair dryer or holding it near a light bulb or radiator. *Never* leave a glob of nose putty sitting on a light bulb, radiator, iron, or other heating element. The results can be devastating.

The basic shape desired is formed directly on the face with the putty, then the edges must be smoothed out to blend with the skin. As additional layers are added, each must be smoothed and blended, so that a hard line will not appear between the false area and the actor's own face (see Figure 14).

Once the final shape has been achieved, the putty can be "set" with an ice cube, if available, or by sprinkling cold water on it. If the putty tends to stick to the fingers during application, a very light coating of cold cream will enable you to smooth and manipulate its surface as desired.

Derma wax or mortician's wax is applied in much the same way as nose putty. Before applying it, however, a coating of spirit gum must be applied to the skin surface to be covered, as the wax does not have the sticky, adhering quality of nose putty. Sometimes, if the actor tends to perspire heavily, it is a good idea to apply spirit gum beneath nose putty, too.

To model the derma wax, it is necessary to dip the fingers in cold water, and occasionally sprinkle the surface with cold water, or rub it with an ice cube, if available. When the desired shape has been obtained, it is necessary to seal the surface with derma wax sealer, which can be obtained from the same firms that sell derma wax, allowing it to dry and harden firmly before applying makeup base.

A good substance for modeling on the face can be made by combining equal parts of derma wax and nose putty, heated in a double boiler. The resulting substance is easier to handle than either of its components alone and, when applied with spirit gum and sealer, gives a greater sense of self-confidence to the actor who must wear it.

The best base makeup to use over nose putty or derma wax is greasepaint. Pancake makeup *can* be used, but must be daubed on with great care, rather than rubbed on with the sponge. If the surface is damp, either from cold cream or water used in the modeling process, the surface must first be powdered.

If any prosthetic device is used, ample time must be allowed for the actor to rehearse wearing it. A false nose, in particular, alters the quality of the vocal timbre, and any device glued onto the face is bound to create a slight feeling of restriction: a vague discomfort or stiffness. Certain actions required by the portrayal of the character might have to be modified to accommodate the added facial structure. A good example can be found in the character of Cyrano de Bergerac, who must be extremely voluble and physically active, all the while wearing an enormous, grotesque nose.

Hair

Throughout history, as men, morals, politics, and life styles have changed, so have fashions changed. One of the most important parts of fashion is the way in which the hair is worn: the amount of hair, the length of it, whether it is false or real, revealed or covered, the addition of or lack of ornamentation. Most good costume books contain valuable descriptions and illustrations of period hair styles, and many companies that supply wigs and costumes for rental or purchase submit style sheets upon request.

Wigs are not the most comfortable accessories to wear, but just as a dedicated actor is willing to wear heavy velvets, wools, and even fur under the intense heat of stage lights, so he must sometimes endure the heat and weight of a wig.

The best theatrical wigs are made of real human hair. Their care and maintenance on a wig block are discussed in Chapter III. Less expensive wigs made of mohair, yak hair, and other substances might be used in special instances, but the lower expense should not deter the actor from taking very good care of them. Some very attractive wigs are now being made of some of the newer synthetic substances, but caution should be used in wearing them in the theatre, as theatrical lighting media, particularly blue, change the color of the synthetic hair mysteriously and alarmingly.

If the wig has natural-looking forehead and ear hairlines, it is quite likely to have pieces of "lace," or lightweight bobbinet netting attached to the front, and to the side flaps that fit down in front of the ears. The lace must be firmly attached to the skin with spirit gum, then foundation makeup blended over the edge of it to conceal the line. For obvious reasons, the wig must be carefully fitted and the instructions sent by the company supplying the wig for measurements followed to the letter.

Whether a fitted wig with lace or one that is not attached with spirit gum is worn, the wig should not be removed backstage during rehearsal or performance. The only way to put it on correctly is to ease it onto the head from front to back, carefully centering it at the forehead line and adjusting it with the help of a mirror. If it is removed to cool the head while the actor is not onstage, then quickly replaced before an entrance, the odds are very good that it will be refitted crookedly, or with the actor's own hair peeking out from underneath.

The care and cleaning of all hairpieces must be kept in mind between rehearsals and performances, as indicated in Chapter III.

It may become necessary to wear smaller hairpieces as adjuncts to the natural hair. Such items as falls, wiglets, chignons, and braids are often worn.

A fall, which is a hank of long (usually shoulder-length) hair, is usually sewn onto a band that circles the head at the crown, just behind the ears, and the nape of the neck. It should be secured to the hair with ample quantities of bobby pins, so that it will not slip back on the head.

To fasten wiglets of curls, chignon or figure-eight buns, and braids to the hair, it is necessary to make an anchor of the actress' own hair by either making tight pin curls or binding the hair in elastic bands. Then the added piece is fastened with wire or plastic hairpins or combs. Experimentation will determine the securest way to anchor hairpieces.

Figure 28 *Equipment for making beards, mustaches, and sideburns, including straightened and unstraightened crêpe hair, spirit gum, scissors, and comb.*

Figure 28 illustrates some of the equipment used in making beards, mustaches, and sideburns. The simplest and least expensive hair to use for the pur-

pose is crêpe hair, available from any company that sells theatrical makeup. It comes in a tight braid threaded through with string. When it is unbraided, it is quite kinky, and, for some purposes, it may be desirable to use it that way. If straight hair is desired, however, it must be straightened well in advance of use. It may be either pressed straight with a steam iron, or soaked with water and stretched between two rigid posts, such as the legs of a chair or the verticals on a stairway bannister.

The surface of the face where the hair is to be applied should be clean and free of makeup. At first, until the actor is thoroughly accustomed to applying hair, he might find it advisable to sketch the boundaries of the beard and mustache on his face with a pencil line or brush dipped in grease liner. Such lines should be removed or covered with base makeup before appearing onstage (see Figure 29).

If spirit gum is used to attach the hair, the area to receive the hair should be painted with a liberal amount of the gum, then allowed partially to dry, until the gum becomes "tacky." Only a small area at a time should be attempted, beginning with the very tip of the chin. It must be remembered that the underside of the chin and the upper part of the throat grow hair when the beard is allowed to grow. Some of the worst amateur efforts at beard-making are those in which the actor has applied hair only to the top of his chin and jawline, forgetting that an audience will see him in profile and certainly notice that there is no hair under the jaw or chin.

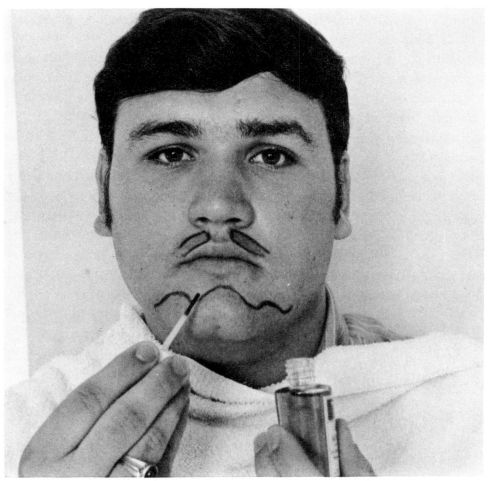

Figure 29 *Missouri Western College student Donald Crabtree has outlined the areas he wishes to cover with crêpe hair, and is now ready to begin applying spirit gum.*

First, a length of the hair is clipped away from the strip and lightly combed. Then, a cone is formed by twisting one end and fanning out the other end of the piece. The cone is attached to the top, sides, and underside of the chin (see Figure 30). Loose hairs should be picked away from the surface with either the fingertips or tweezers.

Then, painting only small areas with gum, and using only small tufts of combed hair, the remainder of the beard, the mustache, and the sideburns are added, building layer upon layer, and working from the center out and from the bottom upward.

You will find you have a shaggy, unkempt beard and mustache (Figure 31). If your character requires such a beard, then your work is finished, with the exception of perhaps stroking the hair into place with your fingertips. More likely, however, the beard will need trimming, which is done with a pair of sharp scissors. You should trim only a very small portion at a time, moving back and forth from one side to the other to achieve balance and symmetry.

Crêpe hair is very dry and lusterless and may tend to be unruly, to "float," or get in the way of your mouth when you speak. A light application of hair tonic, hair cream, or petroleum jelly should control the hair and give it a natural-looking luster. For a "handlebar" mustache with curls at the outer edges, or for a stiff, upward-pointing mustache such as that worn by the famous painter Salvador Dali, you will need to use mustache wax, or *"pomade hongroise,"*

which is available from companies selling theatrical makeup.

In applying a beard and mustache, it is as important to leave certain areas free of hair as to apply hair. Note that there is no hair in the little indentation at the center of the upper lip, nor is there any in the two little crescents at the outer corners of the mouth on the chin.

Spirit gum is rather unpleasant to use, and over a long period of time, continued use is likely to create skin problems. If you expect to wear a beard, mustache, and/or sideburns in many rehearsals and performances, you might prefer to make them on a rubber latex base, which can be reused. The procedure is the same, except that prior to attaching the hair, five or six layers of latex should be painted onto the skin, just enough to make a sturdy shell upon which to build the hairpiece. After the piece or pieces have been constructed, simply peel away the latex, trim the edges of it, and keep it stored in a clean, dry box when not in use. The pieces are reapplied with surgical adhesive.

Sometimes an effect of baldness is required. The ideal solution is the rental or purchase of a special bald wig. Such a wig must be secured in front, below the natural hairline, with spirit gum, then base makeup blended onto it to cover the line between wig and skin. If a "billiard-ball" effect of total baldness is desired, a snug-fitting, smooth-surfaced swimming cap may be used, trimming it to fit smoothly just below the natural hairline all the way around, and securing it with spirit gum, then applying founda-

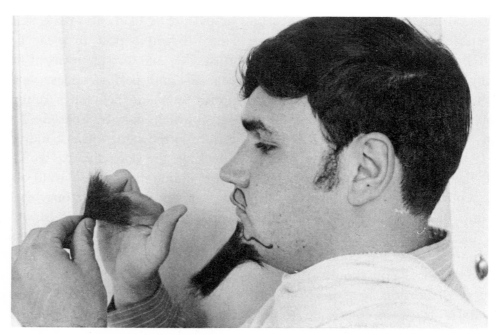

Figure 30 *The actor has applied a cone of crêpe hair to all sides of his chin; in his hands he holds another cone to demonstrate how it is made.*

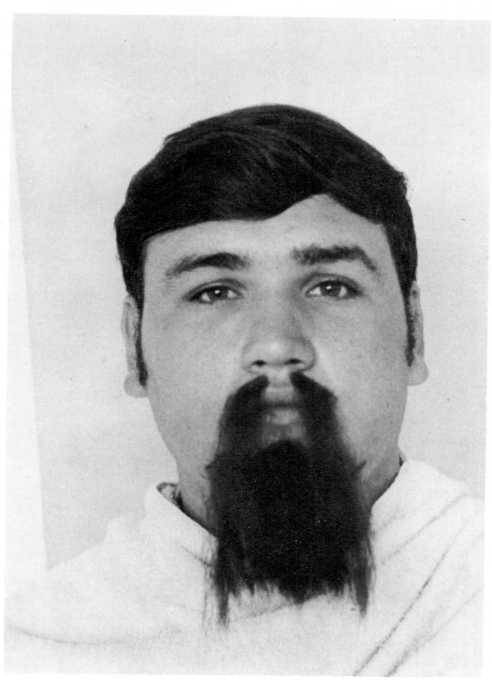

Figure 31 *The hair has been applied to the areas desired, but has not been trimmed or shaped.*

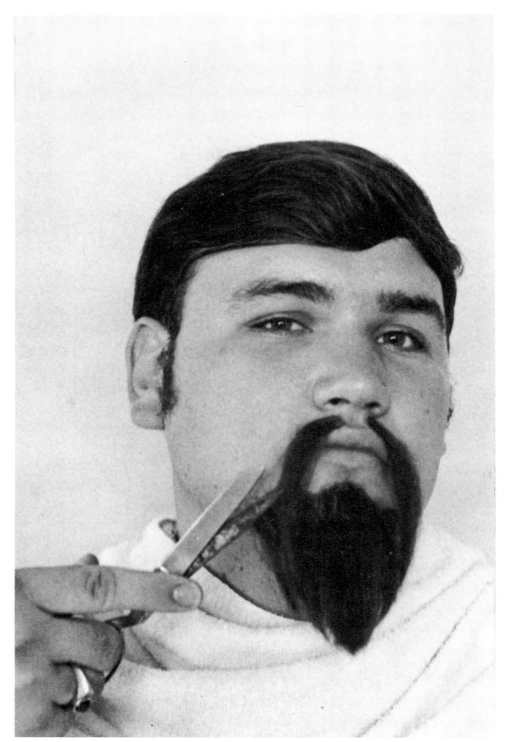

Figure 32 *Mr. Crabtree trims the beard and mustache with scissors. (Photographs by Lynne Anderson)*

tion makeup. If necessary, a fringe of crêpe hair can be added above the ears and around the back of the head.

If a receding hairline or a bald patch at the crown of the head is desired, the hair can be saturated with spirit gum or nonflexible collodion, smoothed and flattened down, and foundation makeup painted liberally over the hard surface. This is really only a makeshift method, extremely messy to clean, and very uncomfortable for the wearer. If the effect is required for more than one or two performances, a suitable wig should be rented or purchased.

If the effect of a one- or two-day "stubble" beard is desired, and the actor's own beard is too light to project from the stage, a "five-o'clock shadow" can be created by cutting dark crêpe hair into tiny pieces, no longer than ⅛", spreading them in a soft towel, then pressing the towel against the chin, jaws, and upper lip, which have been painted with spirit gum.

Crêpe hair comes in a variety of colors and shades. Remember, in purchasing lengths of crêpe hair, that beards and mustaches are not always the same color as a man's hair. Also, several shades can be mixed, such as might be done to obtain an effect of "salt-and-pepper" gray.

Several other uses for spirit gum and surgical adhesive might be found valuable:

1. If jewelry is worn onstage, particularly earrings and bracelets, a touch of spirit gum will prevent them from flying off in violent action or dancing.

2. To prevent embarrassment when wearing a costume with very low decolletage or a strapless bodice, spots of spirit gum or surgical adhesive will contribute to safety and self-confidence.

3. Loose-heeled shoes, such as ballet slippers or open-heeled sandals, can be glued to the heels to prevent stumbling and excess noise.

4. Sequins, rhinestones, silk patches, and other "exotic" additions can be secured to the skin with surgical adhesive (see Figure 6); also animal whiskers made of yarn or broomstraws.

SPECIAL MAKEUP

Although emphasis has been laid upon the makeup of the face, other areas of the body must frequently be made up in order to complete the overall effect of characterization desired. A good rule of thumb is that all exposed areas of the skin must have makeup attention. Naturally included would be the ears, the back of the neck, shoulders, arms and hands, and sometimes the legs and feet.

The hands and arms are probably the most frequently neglected areas of skin to be made up. It is not enough to have a wrinkled face and white hair in portraying an elderly person: The illusion will be ruined if the hands and arms look young. In old age, the veins on the wrists and the backs of the hands become more pronounced; they may be emphasized with medium blue liner. Also, older people develop a pigmentation generally referred to as "liver spots," which are brownish oversized freckles on the hands and arms.

Figure 33 illustrates makeup on the

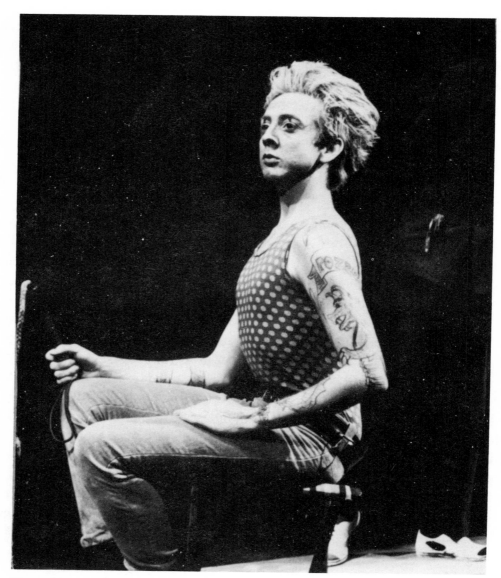

Figure 33 *In* Waiting for Godot *at Memphis State University, an actor displays some imaginative characterization in the makeup on his arm.*

arms in the form of tattoos as a viable element of makeup characterization. Emphasis of the lines on the knuckles will help to indicate aged hands, and if an effect of arthritis or rheumatism is desired, latex and cotton padding may be added to the joints.

A person who has been barefoot in the out-of-doors will naturally have dust or dirt on the tops, as well as the bottoms of the feet. A rustic type with sunburned face whose legs and feet are white and clean will never be credible to an audience.

Sometimes an actor is called upon to play a character whose ethnic or racial background is totally different from his own. In such a case, attention to all exposed skin is tremendously important. It must always be remembered, in darkening the skin, that the palms of the hands and the soles of the feet remain light.

In applying makeup for a Negro character, it must be kept in mind that black skin is as subject to highlights and shadows as lighter skin. As compared to Caucasian makeup, if the actor thinks of his Negro makeup as being the negative of a positive photograph, that mental image may help in creating the emphatic highlights and shadings required for an effective appearance.

One of the most difficult aspects of creating an Oriental makeup is to reproduce the unique shape of the Oriental eye. One of the most old-fashioned ways is the application of fishskins at the corners of the eyes with adhesive, stretching them outward and upward, and attaching them at the temples. Then base makeup is applied over the transparent skins. This is uncomfortable, and not always foolproof, as the stress on the stretched skins may cause them to come loose during a performance.

A more efficacious method is to attach a flap of latex or a strip of adhesive tape (with a thin layer of paper on the adhesive side over the eye itself) to the upper eyelid, carefully trimming it to form the "almond" shape generally associated with the Oriental eye.

On rare occasions, quick changes are required in makeup. Perhaps the classic example is found in *Victoria Regina,* in which the actress playing the Queen of England must believably progress from a young girl to an aged dowager. For such a characterization, hours of rehearsal on makeup alone are required, so that the best possible effect can be achieved in the least time.

Undoubtedly, quick changes of face can best be handled by the use of masks (see Chapter V), although minor changes can be made through touch-ups, and sometimes the exercise of imagination and ingenuity. An example of the latter is found in an opera production, in which the corps de ballet was required to change from circus clowns into realistic villagers in only a few seconds. The villager costumes were worn underneath the voluminous clown costumes, and the "breakaway" makeup was simply painted patches of foot corn and callus plasters, which could be quickly peeled off the face.

A type of production that requires special attention to makeup is the out-of-doors production. As such productions are generally spectacular, and given to the "larger-than-life" treatment in all respects, the makeup will naturally have to go along in style.

The actor in such a production is up against two problems in terms of a choice between natural subtlety or exaggeration: those spectators in the audience sitting an acre or so away and trying to see; those spectators sitting an acre or so away and using field glasses. A general rule is to aim for the middle, with some exaggeration, but not so much that those up close or those using optical aids will find the makeup grotesque.

A frequent problem with out-of-doors productions is bugs. They are a problem to everyone: actor, technician, and spectator. The lights of the amphitheatre tend to intensify the problem. Many commercial preparations are available that can be sprayed or sponged onto the skin to repel insects, but before using them under or over makeup, be sure to test them for oiliness, color, and allergenic potential.

Another problem with out-of-doors productions is rain . . . but if it rains, let's face it, you've had it anyway!

Each theatrical production presents its own unique problems, and each problem must be solved as it comes along, often with considerable brainteasing.

FINAL TOUCHES

Once you have completed your makeup to the satisfaction of yourself and your director, it is time to "set" it for the ultimate appearance onstage.

If you are using dry rouge, it should be applied last, with a soft watercolor brush and carefully blended so that no hard edges will be apparent. If moist rouge is used, it should be applied and blended at the same time as the highlights and shadows of broad areas of the face.

If heavy perspiring has occurred during the application of makeup (and this may well happen, as the bare lights in a dressing room are often hot, and air conditioning is a seldom-found luxury), the excess should be gently blotted away with a dry towel or tissues.

Powder is then applied. The powder should be approximately the same color as the base makeup, or if makeup is being shared on a group basis, the colorless, transparent neutral shade is ideal. A large powder puff is loaded with powder, then pressed against the surface, *not* stroked on, as the latter may smear the lines. The excess powder is then brushed away gently with a powder brush or a baby's hairbrush. Be sure to brush away from the nostrils and eyes, toward the outside edges of the face. Powder should be applied and brushed away to all areas covered with makeup, including hands, arms, shoulders, legs, and feet.

It is a good idea to have a miniature dressing room backstage, where it will be handy to all actors. It should have a minimal source of light, a small mirror, a container of powder with a puff and brush, and a container of tissues. Thus, when a touch-up or blotting of perspiration is needed during a rehearsal or performance, the equipment is close at hand for even the quickest of exits, and the actor does not risk missing a cue by leaving the backstage area to return to his dressing room. The "mini-dressing room" might well contain a pitcher of water and paper cups, too.

Finally, following the rehearsal or performance, a thorough cleaning up is called for. A sign of the worst form of amateurism is to appear in public still wearing theatrical makeup.

Cold cream, mineral oil, commercial cleansing preparations, or common household shortening may be used to remove the makeup. To remove constructions made of nose putty and/or derma wax, a piece of sewing thread or lightweight string, about 6″ long, can be run between the skin and the construction, thus retaining the piece almost intact for future reuse.

The sticky residue of spirit gum can be softened and removed with isopropyl (rubbing) alcohol. A preparation called spirit gum remover is available, but alcohol or fingernail polish remover will work as well. In using any of the preparations, be sure to keep them away from the eyes, nostrils, and mouth.

Rubber latex and surgical adhesive can easily be peeled or rolled away from the skin.

The two final steps in the cleanup process before you go home are: first, a thorough cleaning with soap and water to remove final traces of makeup and the removal preparations; second, you must clean house; all tissues and other trash should be put in a suitable receptacle, makeup and equipment cleaned and put away, and your costume hung up, with accessories put in their proper drawers or on shelves.

If you have given a good performance, based on plenty of preparation and rehearsal in every respect, and if you have looked well to an audience, your sense of achievement should be tremendous. Congratulations!

A REVIEW OF STEPS

As an aid to efficiency in preparing your makeup, a brief checklist follows. Eventually, the orderly application of makeup will become as habitual as the saying of your well-memorized, well-rehearsed lines. But at first it might be a good idea to keep a written list of procedures close at hand while making up. In the long run, it can save you much time and error.

1. Examination of and thorough acquaintance with your own face.
2. Complete understanding of your character.
3. Design of your makeup.
   a. Consultation with director.
   b. Consultation with costumer and electrician.
4. Inventory and ordering of makeup equipment.
5. Experimentation, practice, rehearsal.
6. Complete cleaning of skin to remove all street makeup and soil.
7. Application of prosthetic devices.
8. Marking off of areas to receive adhesive for hair or other materials.
9. Application of base makeup.

10. Application of shadows and highlights to broad areas of face, including moist rouge.
11. Eye makeup.
    a. False eyelashes.
    b. Eye shadow.
    c. Lining.
    d. Mascara.
    e. Eyebrows.
12. Lines and fine highlights.
13. Application of hair.
14. Wig and blending of hairline.
15. Dry rouge and powder.
16. Makeup removal and final cleanup.

The face your audience sees will be a carefully planned blending of your own face and a face made of imagination and research to create the character you are meant to portray. A lot of hard work will go into that face, but as you practice and become adept at the use of the tools available to you, you will increasingly enjoy the real fun that can be yours in the theatre: the joy of artistic creation.

Chapter V

THE OTHER FACE:
MASKS AND MASK-MAKING

"The trumpet sounds: be mask'd; the maskers come."

Shakespeare, *Love's Labour's Lost,*
Act V, Scene ii.

MASKS AS A FORM OF MAKEUP

The mask may be considered a kind of ultimate stage makeup. When an actor or dancer wears a mask, the form and features of his own face no longer affect the appearance he presents to his audience. Limited only by his imagination and skill, the artist mask-maker has free rein to create features that are bold, subtle, realistic, highly stylized, or grotesque. He is not restricted, as is the makeup artist, by the performer's own facial characteristics.

Upon sophisticated contemporary audiences, the mask has an uncanny power not unlike that which it wields over the most primitive peoples. The mystery of watching a mask, rather than the performer's face, is matched by the magical influence that wearing a mask has on the actor or dancer.

Use of masks in the theatre has had a considerable renaissance in this age of psychiatry and psychology, when a person's "real" personality is known to be frequently hidden behind the "false face" he presents to the world. Also, the advent in this century of subsidized repertory companies and of college and school theatre programs has brought about the revival of plays from all periods of the history of the theatre. Hence, masks are often used in modern productions of Greek, Roman, Medieval, Commedia dell' Arte, and Renaissance plays. Also there is today an awakening interest in the Orient and its drama and dance. Masks have been an intrinsic part of Eastern theatre and dance for centuries. An outstanding example is the use of highly stylized masks in the classic Japanese Nō dance-dramas.

By employing masks, as few as two or three actors could play all the major roles in Greek tragic drama. Masks, along with heavily padded costumes and thick-soled boots called cothurnius, served to give those actors majestic size and appearance that lent them the qualities of gods, goddesses, and rulers, so often the chief characters of Greek tragedy. A recent production of Sophocles' *Oedipus Rex* by the Stratford, Ontario Repertory Theatre, which has been filmed, shows excellent examples of the use of the mask in contemporary revivals of classic drama.

The most fascinating aspect of medieval religious and ethical drama was Hell's Mouth, out of which came all kinds of devils, demons, and deadly sins. Those figures were infinitely more appealing to onlookers than the rather boring angels and saints. Elaborate masks were often used in the mystery and morality plays of the Middle Ages to frighten members of the audience toward paths of righteousness. Modern revivals of such medieval-inspired Renaissance plays as Christopher Marlowe's *Dr. Faustus* frequently employ masks for such characters as Lucifer, Beelzebub, and the Seven Deadly Sins.

Commedia dell' Arte actors, portraying such stock characters as the Soldier, the Shepherd, the Harlequin, and the Buffoon, often wore masks with greatly exaggerated features. The tradition may have come from the Roman comedy, which in its turn was influenced by the Greeks.

Masks are sometimes worn by actors in plays by such outstanding twentieth-century playwrights as Eugene O'Neill, Elmer Rice, and Luigi Pirandello. Also,

there has been a revival of mask use in modern dance and ballet presentations.

PRACTICAL CONSIDERATIONS

Regardless of what play or dance is being produced in which masks are to be employed, certain fundamental factors need to be considered.

If the actors who are to wear masks must speak, some way of preventing the masks from muffling their voices must be found. The most obvious solution to the problem is to use one-half or three-quarter masks so that the actor's mouth is not covered. Such a technique was used in the modern production of Euripedes' *Trojan Women* shown in Figure 34. Some theatre historians believe that original full-face Greek tragic masks had built-in megaphones to carry the actor's voice throughout an open amphitheatre, but such constructions would not be suitable to more realistic, less formal contemporary productions of classical plays.

Another solution to the speech problem can be to build full-face masks in two portions. The lower lip, chin, and jaw of the mask can be hinged to the upper part of the mask face, much as in real life. The full-face masks for Eugene O'Neill's *Great God Brown* shown in Figure 35 were so made. Small pieces of the rubber sheeting used by dentists were stretched tautly to join the upper and lower portions of Dion's and Cybel's masks. When the actor spoke, the rubber portions stretched to allow the mask mouths to open; conversely, when the actors were not speaking, the rubber

Figure 34 *Euripedes'* Trojan Women *produced at MacMurray College, Jacksonville, Illinois, 1954.*

sheeting contracted, thereby restoring to the masks the appearance of human facial features at rest. The masks allowed the actors' voices to be heard well, and the moving jaws created an uncannily realistic effect. However, such a method of mask-making is not recommended to any but the most ambitious and patient of mask-makers.

Figure 35 *Eugene O'Neill's* Great God Brown *produced at Smith College, Northampton, Mass., 1950.*

The mask must be durable, for it may be subjected to long and intensive use. However, it must also be lightweight, so as to be worn comfortably and naturally by the actor. Going along with lightness and durability is the necessity for a simple and secure way to be found for attaching the mask to the actor's head or face, although sometimes masks are frankly held in front of the face, at-

tached to a rod or stick like a lorgnette.

Masks must be finished in plenty of time for the actors to have as much practice as possible with their "false faces." Oftentimes very exaggerated bodily movements are employed by the mask-wearer to exploit the features and expression of the mask. At other times, powerful bodily movements must be used by actors or dancers wearing masks in order to compensate for the lack of subtle facial changes that otherwise aid the performer in his characterization. Contrariwise, sometimes a mask-wearer may want to minimize movement or use slow, deliberate motion in order to provide domination by the mask of his character and presence.

The interior of the mask must fit the wearer's features as comfortably and as closely as possible. Such an interior contour may be achieved in two fundamental ways. The first is by using an actual life cast of the actor's face as a basis for mask-building. This technique will be discussed later in detail. Secondly, calipers, an accurate ruler, and full-front and profile photographs of the actor may be used to achieve accurate fittings. The latter method was used with the *Great God Brown* masks, and the portrait quality of the masks may be observed when they are compared to the performers' own features. This method will also be discussed later in more detail. Lining of the mask with felt or velvet will add to the comfort of the wearer, especially when a mask must be frequently worn, or worn for long periods of time.

Lastly, and obviously, the actor or dancer must be able to see when he is wearing his mask. This may not be absolutely mandatory if no movement is required for a particular role, or if the part being played is that of a blind person, but usually masks have eye openings placed in such a way that the wearer can see. The openings may or may not coincide with the eyes of the mask, although they usually do. The eyes are often thought of as a person's most expressive feature, yet as the onlooker sees only empty sockets where the mask eyes would normally be, the eye's appearance is not missed. Strangely, or perhaps magically, the observer seems to supply the eye's expression through use of his own imagination.

PRELIMINARY STEPS

Before making a mask you may want to see actual masks or photographs of masks that have been created by peoples all over the world for religious rites and for dramatic and dance presentations. Most large art museums and museums of natural history have collections of masks that are well worth seeing. You may have the good fortune to live near such an institution. Book and periodical sources for background study are listed at the end of this book, and many of the sources, in turn, have their own bibliographies to help you find still more materials.

A film, *The Loon's Necklace,* makes excellent use of masks in a fascinating portrayal of an Indian legend. The film is widely available, and one source for obtaining it is given at the end of the book. If you live in a city that has a Chinatown, you can see an enormous dragon mask, with an opening and closing mouth, if you attend a Chinese New Year celebration and follow the dragon dance through the streets.

To get the feel of what it is like to be inside a mask, before actually wearing one of your own, you may want to try wearing a simple commercial Halloween mask of pressed paper or rubber. Or a very simple mask may be made almost instantaneously by cutting eye holes in a paper bag and then drawing a few facial features on the paper surface. When you first put on a mask, look inward for a moment and feel the effect that wearing a mask has on you, psychologically. Then look at yourself in a mirror, do a few movements of your head and body, to see the effect a mask may have outwardly on an actor and his audience.

Before getting into more complex mask-making projects you may want to try one or more of the very simple techniques and materials. If so, you will find a separate listing of easy and quick mask-making procedures at the close of this chapter.

SOME FUNDAMENTAL PRINCIPLES

Mask-making is essentially a sculptural art form; therefore, as with sculpture generally, only certain basic techniques may be followed. Sculpture, and therefore mask-making, may be termed either "subtractive" or "additive." Sculpture for many centuries was largely "subtractive," or carving in nature. Michelangelo is probably the greatest accepted master of "subtractive" sculpture. In more recent times, sculptural forms are often first modeled of clay or a similar substance and then the model is cast, probably in plaster. The final sculpture is created by pouring any of a wide variety of materials into the cast-mold. The poured material hardens, the mold is broken away, and the resulting cast sculpture is then refined and finished. This is, then, an "additive" form of sculpture, because the original work is a building up rather than a carving away process.

The "subtractive" carving of masks is an ancient art. Wood is the material most often used for mask-carving, but other substances such as ivory and bone have also been used. Because we are concerned here with masks for the stage, the carving of masks is going to be discounted, because of the earlier mentioned necessities for lightness and inner contour fit. That does not mean that very successful drama and dance masks cannot be, and have not been carved. For example, the very delicate masks for Japanese Nō dance-drama are carved of wood. But the skill required to carve a mask and to make it fit, and still keep it very thin and light, is probably beyond the beginning mask-maker. By all means try carving a mask, if you wish, but this form of "subtractive" sculptural mask-making will not be further pursued here.

Several variations of "additive" sculptural mask-making follow. Any, or combinations of all of them, can be used successfully by the beginning mask-maker.

First of all there must be a design or idea of the mask you intend to create.

Even though a three-dimensional art form is called for, a mask design can quite successfully be done as a drawing, and shading used to suggest the sculptural quality of the mask. Figures 36, and 37 show original sketches for the *Great God Brown* masks of Dion and Cybel. When the photograph of the finished masks is studied (Figure 35), it may be seen that the original designs were considerably modified. Mask designs need not be drawn, they may be carved or made in the third dimension of clay or some other modeling material.

"Additive" Procedures

1. For most "additive" forms of mask-making a cast of the actor's own face, of a life mask, can be a most useful base. Following is a step-by-step series of directions for making a life mask.

a. Explain to the person whose life mask is to be made exactly what procedures are to be followed, and assure him of the safety of this long-used technique.

b. Have at hand the following materials:

Five pounds of plaster
Jar of cold cream or petroleum jelly
Two paper straws or glass tubes
A piece of elastic sewed to a square of fabric or plastic to be stretched around the actor's head to cover his hairline and ears
Another piece of fabric or plastic to go around the actor's neck, under his chin, to catch excess plaster

Figure 36 *Mask design for Eugene O'Neill's* Great God Brown *at Smith College.*

Figure 37 *Mask design for Eugene O'Neill's* Great God Brown *at Smith College. (Photographs by Vince Lopardo)*

A large bucket, basin, or pan
2½ to 3 quarts of cold water
A measuring cup

c. Ask the subject to coat his face liberally with cold cream or petroleum jelly; the eyelids and eyebrows should be quite heavily covered. The cream should be smoothed out so that there are no excessively heavy deposits, but the coating should not be overly thin in any area. Have the actor insert glass or paper tubes into his nostrils, and give him plenty of time to be sure he can breathe through them with his mouth tightly closed. The subject himself, or an assistant, can hold the tubes in place until plaster sets around them. Have the subject lie down on a rigid, flat surface, and elevate his head with a cushion or towel. Make him as comfortable as possible. Arrange the fabric or plastic coverings

so as to keep plaster from flowing or dropping onto any area except the subject's face. A fairly heavy piece of cardboard with an oval hole cut in it to fit around the actor's face, masking off his ears, hairline, and neck can also be used for the purpose of controlling the plaster.

d. Into two to three quarts of *cold* water begin to add plaster, one cup at a time. Constantly stir in the plaster with one hand near the bottom of the bucket until the mixture of plaster and water is the consistency of thin cream. About ten to fifteen cups of plaster will be required. Because it "sets up" or hardens very quickly, the plaster must now be rapidly applied to the subject's face; however, a few preliminary drops on his forehead will help him to know how the substance is going to feel. Then as speedily as possible, apply handfuls of plaster to the subject's face, making sure that the tubes for breathing are held in place and that the subject's eyes and mouth are closed. The plaster should be 1½″ to 2″ thick over the entire face, and indentations on either side of the nose should be filled in so that the outer surface of the mold is smoothly rounded, with no intentional cavities.

It requires approximately fifteen to twenty minutes for the plaster to set (dental plaster hardens in eight to ten minutes). The plaster will get quite warm as it hardens, but it will not burn. It will help to assure the subject that you are nearby, and that there is no danger of plaster burn. Before the plaster hardens, any ragged edges at the bottom of the cast should be somewhat evened out. When the plaster cast begins to cool, it is ready to remove.

e. The cast is removed by spreading the fingers widely over its surface and by grasping it firmly but gently on both sides. Ask the subject to press his head backward as you lift the cast upward off his face. Be sure he keeps his eyes and mouth closed until he has an opportunity to wash off loose particles of plaster from his face at a nearby sink or basin.

Allow the cast to cool and harden *thoroughly*. Then coat the inside with cold cream or liquid nondetergent soap; or mineral oil may be brushed into the mold and petroleum jelly applied over it.

f. Place the negative cast so that it can be filled with a fresh batch of plaster mixed exactly as before. The second batch of plaster is poured into the mold. As you pour the first thin coating, you should blow on it in order to eliminate air bubbles that may form between the two plaster surfaces. Then pour the mold full of the remaining plaster. Allow the second cast to set thoroughly, then gently and carefully break away the negative mold in small pieces with a chisel and mallet.

g. Once the resulting cast is revealed and has been trimmed and smoothed, it is ready to form a basis for a large variety of mask construction possibilities. The fit of the mask is assured, for it will have been built on a cast of the actor's own face. The cast's surface should be coated, when it is thoroughly dry and hard, with several layers of white shellac to prevent its plaster surface from sticking to the final mask.

Because only a very little plaster is used to make both the negative and positive castings, the resulting life mask is quite inexpensive to make. However, the process is intricate and time-consuming.

If exact contours are not required, and if the budget permits, the mask-maker may want to use a "dummy plastic mask" such as the one shown in Figure 38, thus eliminating the need for a life-mask cast. Such masks are made according to the relatively standard proportions of the human face and should provide adequate fitting.

Whether a life-mask cast, or a "dummy plastic mask" is used, the resulting positive casts, when plaster is poured into the negative molds, are much alike. Figure 38 shows a positive full-face cast being removed from a "dummy plastic mask," but the effect would be the same if it were being removed from a rather thicker plaster life cast, the making of which was described in detail above.

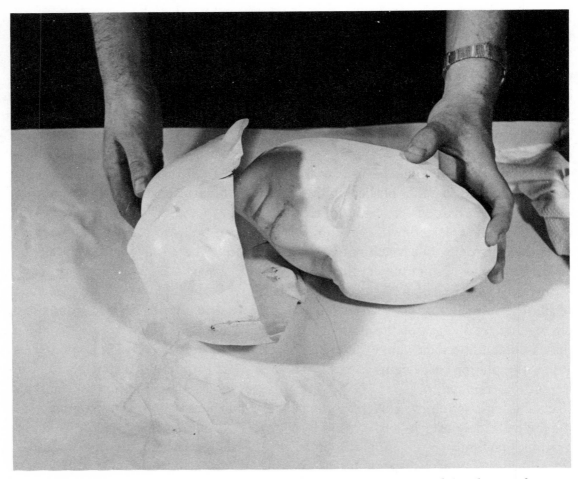

Figure 38 *Full-face mask being removed from "dummy plastic mask." (Photograph courtesy of Polymer Corporation, Ltd., Sarnia, Ontario, Canada)*

2. Figure 39 shows how the basic life mask or "dummy plastic mask" casts can be altered with clay to exaggerate, distort, or otherwise change the original features. Any clay may be used, but a plastilina clay, which will not dry out or crack, and which may be used over and over again, is usually the choice of sculptors and experienced mask-makers. The altered plaster cast finally becomes a mask when it is covered with papier-mâché or any of a growing variety of colloid-treated materials, or synthetic rubber materials. In Figure 40, the altered cast is being covered by a new sheet synthetic rubber product called Polysar XB-407, which needs only to be mildly heated to make it pliant. As this material cools it becomes rigid and very light in weight. However, Polysar, as well as Bixnap, Celastic, and other commercial products, are expensive, and usually must be ordered from special supply houses.

Although slower to use, papier-mâché is cheapest and easiest to obtain. Any relatively heavy paper, such as paper toweling, torn into strips and soaked in wallpaper paste (which has been mixed according to package instructions), may be used for this method of mask construction. Some of the most beautiful and long-lasting of masks ever made were constructed of papier-mâché. For that reason, and because the material is so cheap and easily obtainable, the papier-mâché method will be described here in detail.

a. Pieces of aluminum foil will help prevent clay alterations from sticking to the papier-mâché.

b. Tear, do *not* cut, ½″ strips of paper toweling and put strips *one at a time* into wallpaper paste. It is helpful to use two colors of toweling in two sep-

arate batches of paste. Allow time for the paper to absorb all the paste possible.

c. Take strips of paper, one color at a time, from the paste and draw through the fingers to remove excess deposits of paste.

d. Cover the surface of the cast completely with overlapping strips of paper running generally in one direction only. Allow the paper to extend 1″ or 1½″ beyond what would normally be the mask's edge. The paper surface should be kept wet and slippery.

e. Reversing the direction of the

Figure 39 *Clay modeling on positive facial cast.* (*Photograph courtesy of Polymer Corporation, Ltd., Sarnia, Ontario, Canada*)

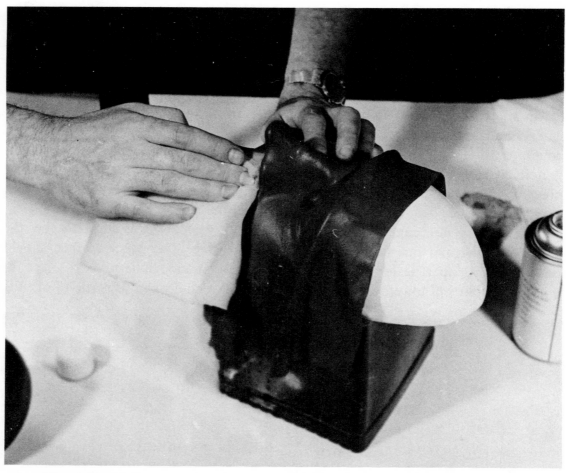

Figure 40 *Making a mask with Polysar XB-407. (Photograph courtesy of Polymer Corporation, Ltd., Sarnia, Ontario, Canada)*

strips, and using the other color of paper, cover the surface of the cast with a second layer. Changing color each time, four or five layers of paper are to be built up in this manner. The two colors show readily if a place has been missed in the placing of the paper strips.

f. If further modifications of contour are to be made, the cheek, brow, or nose lines made more exaggerated, it may be done now by using wadding made of papier-mâché, which is then held in place by crisscrossed layers of paper strips. A total of eight layers of paper will result in a final mask sufficiently strong for

stage use, yet the mask will be very light in weight. Until all the layers of paper are in place, the mask should never be allowed to dry out.

g. Several days may be required for the mask to dry completely. Any artificial heat used to hasten the drying process should be mild, such as an infrared lamp, because too much heat or too quick drying will warp and distort the shape of the mask.

h. After the mask is thoroughly dry, remove it from the cast. In order to remove it, it may be necessary to cut it with a pointed X-acto knife in a place or two. If that is the case, such slits can be easily repaired with a few strips of papier-mâché. With very sharp scissors, trim the edge of the mask to the desired contour and bind the edge with either bias cloth or paper strips. Using a pointed X-acto knife, cut out the eyes, nostrils, and mouth openings. As necessary, bind and finally shape the openings. After the mask is thoroughly dry once more, the surface can be lightly sanded, or a superbly smooth surface may be achieved by coating the mask with gesso, a plaster-based finishing mixture.

i. When the mask surface is refined and dry it should be coated with four or five coats of white shellac, inside and out. Shrinkage and warpage are thereby prevented, and the mask surface is preserved.

j. After the shellac has dried, the mask is ready for painting and finishing. Oil or casein paints give richly textured and durable surfaces. Painting the mask with oils is a slower process and the drying time is longer than with caseins; oils, however, dry to a more permanent finish than do casein colors. The final painting of a mask may be bold or subtle, bright or pale, smooth or textured. When painting it, keep in mind the eventual use of the mask. Tremendously detailed painting will be lost if masks are to be viewed from a considerable distance. The lighting under which masks are to be worn should always be considered in their painting.

k. Headpieces, hair, and all manner of other materials may be required to give the finishing details to a mask.

l. The means whereby a mask is held in place are many. A hat or helmet or wig may be attached to a mask in such a way that an actual headmask is formed. Or holes can be cut, and elastic inserted to hold the mask in place; the elastic can be colored or covered to blend with the actor's hair and will be virtually invisible. The earpieces of spectacles can be built into the final layers of paper, and will hold a relatively lightweight mask in place. Masks may be fastened to sticks or rods and be frankly held before the face, especially for masquerade and period pieces.

m. Once the basic mask form has been made, a whole series of identical masks can be created by simply repeating the above process. The effect of multiple identical masks onstage can be most powerful when a particular play suggests such a phenomenon. In Elmer Rice's *The Adding Machine*, multiple masks might well be strikingly used. Figure 41 shows how multiple identical masks made of Polysar XB-407 were used in a Canadian Opera Company production of *Tales of Hoffmann* as produced in the O'Keefe Centre in Toronto, Canada.

3. There probably exist as many variations on the above technique for mask-making as there are mask-makers. Sometimes the basic cast is entirely dispensed with and a hemispheric plaster or clay base is used upon which facial features are modeled in clay. Front and profile photographs of the actor who is to wear the mask will help to ensure eventual fit when used together with caliper measurements, which have been taken of the wearer's face.

Figure 41   *Act 1 of Offenbach's* Tales of Hoffmann, *produced in the O'Keefe Centre, Toronto, Canada. (Photograph courtesy of Polymer Corporation, Ltd., Sarnia, Ontario, Canada)*

Certain "average" proportions of human features are helpful to know when modeling a mask directly:

	Men	Women
From eyebrow to tip of chin	6″	5⅛″
From apex of occiput to tip of chin	10¾″	9¾″
Width through temples	6¾″	5¾″
Width of jaws	5⅞″	4¾″

Papier-mâché may be built directly over clay just as it can be built over a plaster cast. *Masks and Mask Makers* by Hunt and Carlson[10] describes one such process in considerable detail, as do other sources listed at the end of the book. Although the initial process is the same, Celastic, Bixnap, liquid rubber compounds, Polysar XB-407, leather,

---

[10] Kari Hunt and Bernice Welk Carlson, *Masks and Mask Makers* (New York: Abingdon, 1961), pp. 58–69.

and still other materials can also be used for mask-making. With each special product will come directions for that material's use.

Every mask-maker eventually discovers the material and technique best suited to his designs. The list of references at the end gives as wide a variety as possible of mask-making processes and materials. Many of the references, in turn, list books and articles that suggest even further variations of mask-making techniques.

4. One final form of an "additive" sculptural process, which has application to mask-making, is the wire armature method. The *Great God Brown* masks (Figures 35, 36, 37) were made in that way and the technique is discussed in some detail in *Masks* by Benda.[11]

A coil of soft galvanized wire, approximately 20 gauge, wire cutters, solder, and a small soldering iron are required for the process. The technique is definitely related to contemporary metal sculpture in which shapes are formed by welding or soldering.

a. Careful face and head measurements, plus front and profile photographs of the subject, should be at hand.

b. An oval shape of wire, which is to make the outer contour of the mask, is bent in the proper shape to fit loosely around the wearer's face, and the ends are slightly overlapped and soldered.

c. Then, using the photographs and measurements, a single piece of wire is shaped to form the mask profile, and this piece of wire, in its turn, is soldered appropriately to the oval frame. Then the brow line is initially shaped of still another piece of wire, which is soldered to both the outside oval and profile wires.

d. Gradually, the principal cheek, chin, forehead, and nose contours are formed with wire that has been soldered into place until a face made up of a network of wires is complete.

Then, using a technique similar to that described in the making of a papier-mâché mask, gradually, section by section, the wire forms are covered with paper strips that have been soaked in paste. Once the paper surface is complete and sufficiently thick, the mask is allowed to dry; it is then finished and painted in much the same manner as is an ordinary papier-mâché mask. There is no reason Bixnap, Polysar XB-407, or some other material cannot be used in place of paper and paste, once the wire armature is ready to be covered.

THE MASK WORKSHOP

It would be a very strange theatre indeed that would provide a special room for the sole purpose of making masks. However, they do have to be made *somewhere,* and certain conditions for their execution are necessary.

The chances are, in making masks, you will be assigned to some remote corner of the shop where scenery and props are made, or possibly an area in the wardrobe room or a dressing room. You may even find yourself working right in the middle of the stage, with scenery and lighting

---

[11] W. T. Benda, *Masks* (New York: Watson Guptill, 1944).

grips, stage managers, and property crew people working all around you.

If it is necessary to make a life mask, or several of them, you must have a firm surface large enough for an actor to lie down upon: probably a large work table. You will need such a table anyway for your further work on any type of mask. It should be protected from damage by plastic, scrap wood, or some other material available to you.

You should also make sure that you are within reasonable distance of a source of running water, both for mixing materials and cleaning up. Ventilation is *extremely* important in the use of some of the newer plastic and chemical materials. The solvents that make them pliable, such as acetone, toluol, and other volatile substances must be used with great care in the presence of plenty of fresh air and no flames.

You must also find a place to store the materials you use, once again observing fire precautions, and a safe place to store your work-in-progress, as well as the finished masks. Masks are very much like hats: people who find them would almost not be human if they did not want to try them on. Unauthorized pranksters playing with your masks can well destroy them long before they are ready to be used in the theatre.

Variations of the human face are infinite; not even so-called identical twins look exactly alike. The variety of possible facial forms and expressions is increased even more by the use of stage makeup and masks.

Whatever method of mask-making you may elect to try, you will be taking part in one of the most ancient of all theatrical arts. Somewhere in the clouded origins of drama and dance, when religion and art were one, the making and wearing of masks had their beginnings. With the creation of your own masks you will be making your own contribution to the art and mystery of the mask.

BIBLIOGRAPHY AND FILMOGRAPHY

Some of the following books, periodical articles, and films should be available in your local school or public library.

Your librarian can help you in obtaining other source materials on interlibrary loan; periodical articles not locally available may usually be purchased on photocopy for 10¢ a page.

GENERAL MAKEUP

Books

Baird, John F. *Makeup, A Manual for the Use of Actors, Amateur and Professional.* New York: Samuel French, 1936.

Bamford, T. W. *Practical Makeup for the Stage.* London: Sir Isaac Pitman and Sons, Ltd., 1959.

Berk, Barbara. *First Book of Stage Costume and Make-up.* New York: Franklin Watts, Inc., 1954.

Boublik, Vlastimil. *Art of Make-up for Stage, Television and Film.* Elmsford, New York: Pergamon Publishing Co., 1968.

Cass, Carl B. *Make-up for the Stage.* Cincinnati, Ohio: National Thespian Society.

Chalmers, Helena. *The Art of Make-up for the Stage, the Screen, and Social Use.* New York: D. Appleton and Co., 1925.

Corey, Irene. *Mask of Reality: An Approach to Design for the Theatre.* Cloverlot, Kentucky: Anchorage Press, 1968.

Corson, Richard. *Stage Makeup.* New York: Appleton-Century-Crofts, 1967.

Emerald, Jack. *Make Up in Amateur Movies, Drama, and Photography.* Hastings-on-Hudson, New York: Morgan and Morgan, Inc., 1966.

Gall, Ellen M., and Leslie H. Carter. *Modern Make-up.* San Francisco: Banner Play Bureau, 1928.

Lane, Yoti. *Stage Make-Up.* Minneapolis, Minnesota: The Northwestern Press, 1950.

Liszt, Rudolph. *The Last Word in Make-up.* New York: Dramatists Play Service, Inc., 1960.

Max Factor's Hints on the Art of Make-Up. Hollywood: Max Factor Makeup Studio, 1946, nine pamphlets.

Melvill, Harald. *The Magic of Makeup by the Most Modern Methods for Stage and Screen.* New York: Theatre Arts Books, 1967.

Morton, Cavendish. *The Art of Theatrical Make-up.* London: Adam and Charles Black Co., 1909.

Nack, F. W. *Make Up Book for Professionals.* Chicago: F. W. Nack Co., n.d.

Perrottet, Philippe. *Practical Stage Make-up.* New York: Reinhold Book Corp., 1967.

Strenkovsky, Serge. *The Art of Make-Up.*

New York: E. P. Dutton and Co., 1937.

Thomas, Charles. *Make-up: The Dramatic Student's Approach*. New York: Theatre Arts Books, 1965.

Periodicals

Bowers, F. "Makeup: The Reality of Illusion; Performer Becomes What He Is Not," *Opera News,* 31:8–12, March 11, 1967.

Byrne, M. St. Clare. "Make-Up," *The Oxford Companion to the Theatre,* London: Oxford University Press, 1964. pp. 498–509.

Corson, Richard. "Achieving a Likeness," *Players Magazine,* 28:156, April, 1952.

——— "Makeup Department," *Players Magazine,* 30:34, November, 1953.

——— "More Character—Fewer Lines," *Players Magazine,* 29:178–9, May, 1953.

——— "Practice Techniques," *Players Magazine,* 29:130–31, March, 1953.

Kepros, Nicholas, "Teaching Make-Up," *Theatre Crafts,* 3:12–15; 37–8, October, 1969.

Plaut, G. "New Role of the Makeup Man," *Look,* 29:54–6, February 23, 1965.

SPECIAL MAKEUP

Books

Kehoe, Vincent J.-R., S.M.A. *The Technique of Film and Television Make-up.* London: Focal Press, 1957.

Smith, Dick, S.M.A. *Do-It-Yourself Monster Make-Up Handbook.* New York: Warren Publishing Co., 1965.

Periodicals

Corson, Richard. "Casting Plaster for Rubber Prosthesis," *Players Magazine,* 25:57, December, 1948.

——— "Corrective Technique," *Players Magazine,* 29:88, January, 1953.

——— "Making a Blind Eye," *Players Magazine,* 27:153, April, 1951.

——— "Oriental Eyes," *Players Magazine,* 29:154–5, April, 1953.

——— "Rubber Makeup," *Players Magazine,* 25:34–6, November, 1948.

——— "Stylization," *Players Magazine,* 29:110–1, February, 1953.

Cranzano, Joe. "Creating the Make-up for *The Apple Tree*," *Theatre Crafts,* 1:6–11, March/April 1967.

Smith, Warren, "At Close Range," *Players Magazine,* 30:162, April, 1954.

——— "Tooth Enamel," *Players Magazine,* 31:16, October, 1954.

Vest, Peter J. and Melvin R. White. "Character Makeup for TV," *Players Magazine,* 34:136, December, 1957.

——— "Eye Makeup for Television," *Players Magazine,* 33:138, March, 1957.

——— "Eyelashes for TV," *Players Magazine,* 34:14, October, 1957.

——— "Introduction to TV Makeup," *Players Magazine,* 33:81, January, 1957.

——— "Lip Makeup," *Players Magazine,* 33:184, May, 1957.

——— "Straight and Corrective Makeup for Television," *Players Magazine,* 33:161, April, 1957.

——— "Television Foundation Makeup," *Players Magazine,* 33:102–3, February, 1957.

WIGS AND HAIR

Periodicals

Corson, Richard. "Beards and Mustaches," *Players Magazine,* 28:18, October, 1951.

——— "Effective Use of Wigs," *Players Magazine,* 28:46–7, November, 1951.

DeMann, Ronald. "There's More to Wigs

than Hair," *Theatre Crafts,* 2:34–8, November/December, 1968.

Prisk, Berneice, Ed. "How Many Hair [sic] to Make a Wig," *Players Magazine,* 29:112–3, February, 1953.

Schulte, Charles J.-T., "Hair Makeup," *Players Magazine,* 32:114–5, February, 1956.

———— "How Wigs Are Made," *Players Magazine,* 32:86, January, 1956.

———— "Materials for Hair," *Players Magazine,* 32:34, November, 1955.

———— "White Haired Boy in the Arena," *Players Magazine,* 30:18–9, October, 1953.

———— "Wigs," *Players Magazine,* 32:15, October, 1955.

Smith, Warren, "Rubber Based Beards," *Players Magazine,* 30:185, May, 1954.

Vest, Peter J., and Melvin R. White. "Hair Pieces, Toupees, Wigs," *Players Magazine,* 34:29–30, November, 1957.

BACKGROUND STUDY OF MASKS

Books

Baranski, Matthew. *Mask Making: Creative Methods and Techniques.* Worcester, Massachusetts: Davis, 1954. pp. 99–101.

Benda, W. T. *Masks.* New York: Watson Guptill, 1944. pp. 1–8.

Hunt, Kari and Bernice Welk Carlson. *Masks and Mask Makers.* New York: Abingdon, 1961.

Kniffin, Herbert Reynolds. *Masks.* Peoria, Illinois: Manual Arts Press, 1931. pp. 19–46; 123–35.

Ray, Dorothy Jean. *Eskimo Masks: Art and Ceremony.* Seattle, Washington: University of Washington Press, 1967.

Riley, Olive L. *Masks and Magic.* New York: Studio Publications and Thomas Y. Crowell, 1955.

Slade, Richard. *Masks and How to Make Them.* London: Faber and Faber, 1964.

Periodicals

Anon. "Japanese Masks," *Design,* 66:22–4, November, 1964.

Givens, Sean. "The Mask Makers," *Craft Horizons,* 13:8–12, January, 1953.

King, Eleanor. "The Magic of Masks," *Dance Magazine,* 37:34–7, August, 1963.

Mason, J. Allen. "Primitive Masks from Key Marco, Florida," *Archeology,* 4:4–5, March, 1951.

Shapiro, Harry L. "Magic of the Mask," *New York Times Magazine,* 26–8, April 15, 1951.

SIMPLE PROJECTS IN MASK CONSTRUCTION

Books

Baranski, Matthew. *Mask Making: Creative Methods and Techniques.* Worcester, Massachusetts: Davis, 1954. pp. 1–31.

Cummings, Richard. *101 Masks: False Faces and Make-Up for All Ages and All Occasions.* New York: McKay, 1968.

Grater, Michael. *Paper Faces.* New York: Taplinger, 1967.

Lewis, Shari and Oppenheimer, Lillian. *Folding Paper Masks.* New York: E. P. Dutton, 1965.

Mattil, Edward. *Meaning in Crafts.* Englewood Cliffs, New Jersey: Prentice-Hall, 1965. pp. 150–7.

Periodicals

Anon. "Balloon Masks," *Design,* 61:56, November, 1959.

———— "Simplified Masks: 40 Minute

Project, from Start to Finish," *Design,* 54:133, March, 1953.

Christensen, Ethel M. "Rice, Flour, Sawdust, Make Sculpture Mâché," *School Arts,* 60:30, September, 1960.

Danielson, Phyllis. "Aluminum Maskmaking," *Design,* 65:195, May, 1964.

Jenkins, Jean Foster. "Masks," *School Arts,* 67:38–9, November, 1967.

McCaughey, Gladys. "Excelsior Masks," *Design,* 69:31, Spring, 1968.

Roe, Lois Smethurst. "Secret of Creative Mask Design," *Design,* 67:28–30, September, 1965.

COMPLEX PROJECTS IN MASK CONSTRUCTION

Books

Cummings, Richard. *101 Masks: False Faces and Make-Up for all Ages and All Occasions.* New York: McKay, 1968.

Hunt, Kari, and Carlson, Bernice Welk. *Masks and Mask Makers.* New York: Abingdon, 1961. pp. 58–69.

Kniffin, Herbert Reynolds. *Masks.* Peoria, Illinois: Manual Arts Press, 1931. pp. 56–115.

Powell, Doane. *Masks and How to Make Them.* Pelham, New York: Bridgman, 1948.

Slade, Richard. *Masks and How to Make Them.* London: Faber and Faber, 1964. pp. 44–47.

Periodicals and Unpublished Papers

Anon. "Mask Project in Celastic," *Design,* 56:32–3, September, 1954.

Ehrke, Ernest B. "Mask-Making Is Exciting," *Recreation,* 44:257–60, October, 1950.

Haehl, Chez J. "Paper Mache Masks," *Players Magazine,* 27:157–9, May, 1951.

Mulhare, Mirth T. "Hector Ubertalli, A Maker of Masks," *American Artist,* 25:43–7, October, 1961.

Park, Ralph Kennedy. "Constructing Plastic-Ceramic Masks for Stage Use, Part I," *Players Magazine,* 33, February, 1957.

——— "Constructing Plastic-Ceramic Masks for Stage Use, Part II," *Players Magazine,* 33, March, 1957.

Sniderman, Michael D. "Making Stage Props from Polysar XB-407," Eastern Michigan University, private collection of Lynne Anderson.

FILMS ON MAKEUP*

"Character Make-up for Men," University of Minnesota, 17 minutes.**

"Creative Make-Up for the School Stage," Sigma Educational Films, Box 1235, Studio City, California, set of six 35 mm. filmstrips.

"Make-Up—Straight and Old Age," University of Wisconsin, 20 minutes.**

"Make-Up for Boys," Robert Edmonds, International Film Bureau, 11 minutes.**

"Make-Up for Girls," Robert Edmonds, International Film Bureau, 10 minutes.**

"Make-Up for the Theater," University of California, 13 minutes.**

"Making Theatrical Wigs," University of California, 11 minutes.**

"Stage Make-Up: Youthful Roles," Frangor Films, Coronet Films, 13 minutes.**

"Theory of Make-Up for the Theater," University of California, 7 minutes.**

* Films may be obtained from institution mentioned, or those designated ** may be obtained from Visual Aids Service, Division of University Extension, University of Illinois, Champaign, Illinois 61820.

FILMS ON MASKS*

"Buma: African Sculpture Speaks," Henry R. Cassirer, Encyclopedia Britannica Films, 9 minutes.**

"How to Make a Mask," Ruby Niebauer, Bailey Film Service, 10 minutes.**

"Loon's Necklace," Crawley Films, Canada,

Encyclopedia Britannica Films, or Audio-Visual Services, Pennsylvania State University, University Park, Pennsylvania 16802; 10 minutes.**

"Masks," Pegasus Films, Film Associates of California, 12 minutes.**

"Oedipus Rex," McGraw-Hill/Contemporary Film Rentals, 330 West 42nd Street, New York, N.Y. 10036.

"Paper in the Round," Young America Films, 11 minutes.**

"Paper Mache (Rediscovery Series)" A.C.I. Productions, 14 minutes.**

* Films may be obtained from institution mentioned, or those designated ** may be obtained from Visual Aids Service, Division of University Extension, University of Illinois, Champaign, Illinois 61820.